Planets & Human Life

Planets & Human Life

A Research Work on The Impact of

The Nine Planets on Human Life

Author

Ajay Srivastava

Jyotirvid, Jyotirvisharad

First Edition, 2026

Published by:

Ajay Kumar Srivastava

45, Awas Vikas Colony, Betiya Hata,

Gorakhpur – 273001 (U.P.), India

Mobile No.: +91-9867837184

Lord Ganesha

Prayer

ॐ नमो सिद्धि विनायकाय सर्व कार्य कर्त्रे सर्व विघ्न प्रशमनाय

सर्व राज्य वश्यकरणाय सर्वजन सर्वस्त्री पुरुष आकर्षणाय

श्रीं ॐ स्वाहा ।।

|| Om Namo Siddhi Vinayakaya Sarva kaarya kartrey Sarva vighna prashamnay Sarvarjaya Vashyakarnaya Sarvajan Sarvastree Purush Aakarshanaya Shreeng Om Swaha ||

(**Translation**: O Lord of Wisdom and Happiness, only you make every endeavor and everything possible. You are the remover of all obstacles and you have enchanted every being in the Universe, you are the Lord of all women and all men, Om Swaha.)

Dedication

I dedicate this book to my father (Late) Sri Ram Ashrey Lal Srivastava who taught me to be an independent, courageous and determined person, and my mother Maya Srivastava whose unconditional love and support always help me to overcome all the obstacles in my life. She has a selfless spirit and served others throughout her life. Her immense patience is peerless and she always inspires me to go ahead.

Preface

Planets play a significant role in astrology and have a profound impact on our lives. These celestial bodies influence us right from our birth. I am not participating in the debate on whether these planets affect our lives or not. These subtle energies can only be understood through experience. When a person puts his hand on fire, then he has the experience of burning; there is no discussion that fire burns. If someone says against this, then we can say that get some experience, then come, and we will talk about it. The fire is present; it is visible to the eyes, so there is no difficulty in getting the experience.

But the energies of the planets are not visible to us. Therefore, those who can see only the gross deny the subtle. There is no laboratory in the world where we can test the impact of the energies of these planets on human life. The only way to get experience is to sit in meditation and get some experience. When a person gets experience, they do not get into this useless debate about whether the planets influence us or not. Now he feels the warmth of the fire and knows that the planetary energies exist.

When a person realizes that these moving planets record our every action, then their wrong deeds stop automatically. In the present times, we can understand this by taking the example of a camera recording. God has created nine cameras, i.e., nine planets in the sky, to record the activities of every human being. This means that our every activity is being recorded from nine different angles.

For example, some robbers decide to rob a house and start planning it months in advance. But when they reach the house on the decided day, they are surprised to see that the house is surrounded by heavily armed guards. They all get caught, and these robbers are even more surprised when they see the recording of their every move. How is this possible? This may not be possible in the mundane world, but astrology says it is possible, and it is happening.

These moving planets record our every thought and action. They have the record of our many births, and it can never be erased. Therefore, every person is responsible for their own karma.

This book explains the functioning of the nine planets and how they affect us. While writing this book, I have taken some material from my earlier books with some additions.

I am very much thankful to Mr. Milan Banerjee Editor-Bhagyalipi & Planets and Forecast for providing help and stuff of his father Dr. Nimai Banerjee without which the existence of this is not possible.

I bow down to God for completing this book. Without the grace of the Almighty, it is not possible for me to express my thoughts in words.

Ajay Srivastava

July 25, 2025

Acknowledgement

The existence of this book would not have been possible without the help of my wife Seema and my daughter Saanvi. They provided me enough help to write down my thoughts which I have collected so far in my life. My wife has been instrumental as an illustrator and proof-reader and has given me enough insights to write the matter in a simple and explanatory manner.

Ajay Srivastava

Contents

Chapter 1

Influence of Planets

India has a rich heritage of astrology for thousands of years. It is an art as well as a science that studies the position of planets and the impact of their transit on Earth. These celestial bodies affect human life in many ways, and from time to time, ancient sages have imparted their knowledge to mankind about them.

Astrology has always been a subject of keen interest for those who look up to the sky and want to understand the various nuances of life. This knowledge explains the relationship between humans and the universe. This is the science that studies the influence of planets and stars on human tendencies, their likes and dislikes, their thoughts and behaviour, and their overall life.

Although it is very difficult to assess human behaviour and nature, and it is a subject of behavioral science, astrology can provide guidance in this regard. The science of astrology is not just to provide answers to some trivial worldly questions, but it deals with the most basic questions of life – "*Where do we come from and what is the meaning of life and death*". This question leads man to explore the planets and stars in the sky above, and one day, the light is born within him. Hence, astrology is called the Science of Light.

Hindu astrology considers the influence of nine planets and excludes Uranus, Neptune, and Pluto. Humans are always curious about the future, and astrology tells us how the energies of these nine planets affect us. However, this is not a visible energy that can be seen, felt, or tested in a laboratory. But a rational-minded person cannot ignore its presence simply because it cannot be tested in a laboratory.

For example, if the power of Saturn could be tested in a laboratory, then the results of the test papers would become more important than Saturn itself. However, this will never happen; the effects of these planets on human life can never be tested in a laboratory because they are beyond the limits of our minds. *One who has the ability to test limits cannot test the power that is limitless and infinite.*

These nine planets control the life of every person and give their results according to the karma done by the person. Therefore, every person is responsible for bearing the fruits of his own karma. Bad karma cannot be offset by good karma; it means negative karma cannot be erased by positive karma.

For example, two good karma and two bad karma cannot become zero. The person has to bear the fruits of both good karma and bad karma. Planets in the birth chart and transits produce such positive and negative results, and astrology is the science of studying them.

Every person's birth chart is unique, as the planets and constellations were present in the sky at the time of our birth. Astrology says that the combination of planets and constellations is unique every time and this combination will never happen again in this universe. So, every person is unique in itself, and it is never repeated.

This uniqueness gives us dignity. Nature gives dignity to every human being, but man considers himself poor and does not respect this dignity. People like to copy others by keeping their dignity aside. Astrology teaches us to live a dignified life because this dignity is given to us by nature. Everything is in order and connected here, and ancient scriptures say that even a leaf is affected by the planets and constellations in distant space.

The knowledge of astrology helps in removing disorder from our lives because everything here is in harmony. It helps in achieving the ultimate goal of life, and one can fulfill one's purpose only when they understand that everything here is connected. The concept of harmony of the universe indicates a state of balance, order, and interconnectedness within it.

It also indicates a dynamic equilibrium, where various forces and elements interact and adjust to maintain stability. This harmony is not static but a dynamic process of balance and evolution. Some philosophies, like Taoism, emphasize living in harmony with nature and the universe.

This harmony gives rise to a rhythm where everything in nature seems to be happening on its own. One who flows with this harmony finds infinite bliss. Therefore, every harmony and synchronicity with nature is a step towards achieving it. The knowledge of astrology teaches us to find this harmony where everything flows in a continuous flow.

Bhagavad Gita says:

अहं सर्वस्य प्रभवो मत्तः सर्वं प्रवर्तते ।
इति मत्वा भजन्ते मां बुधा भावसमन्विताः ।।
(Chapter-10, Verse-8)

|| aham sarvasya prabhavo mattah sarvam pravartate

iti matvâ bhajante mâm budhâ bhâva-samanvitâh ||

Translation: I am the origin of all creation. Everything proceeds from Me. The wise who know this perfectly worship Me with great faith and devotion.

Chapter 2

The Cosmic Man

The human body is very mysterious, but there is a sequence to it. The human body is 70% water, and lean muscles contain more water than fatty tissues. On average, muscle tissue contains about 75% water, while fatty tissues contain about 10% water. The body has a strong structure of bones and a network of nerves or vessels. These nerves are intertwined through plexuses that form peripheral nerves; the central nervous system has a special blood supply. Nerves and bones in the body are surrounded by fat, and then, on the outer surface of the body, there are hair and nails.

The same structure exists in the solar system as well. Ancient scriptures say that the human body is a miniature of the cosmic system. "Yatha Pinde Tatha

Brahmande" is a Sanskrit aphorism from ancient Indian philosophy that carries profound significance. It implies that "whatever exists outside of you also exists within you," or that "your body is a microcosm (miniature universe)." The individual (the microcosm) is a reflection of the entire universe (the macrocosm). Every principle, element, and law that governs the vast universe also exists–albeit on a smaller scale–within the human body and mind.

The Siddha system of medicine says nature is man, man is nature. Man has been called the microcosm and the universe the macrocosm. The planets in the universe are related to body parts - Sun-heart, Moon-brain, Mercury-lungs, Jupiter-liver, Saturn-spleen, Mars-gall bladder. The Sun represents the soul, and the soul needs a body to manifest because the soul is invisible. Hence, it has taken birth on the planet Earth. This earth has a satellite, "Moon", which is the fastest moving among the nine planets, and the closest planet is Venus. In astrology, Venus represents fresh water, and the Moon represents salt water. We drink fresh water, which turns into saline water inside the body.

Then the nearest planets to Earth are Mercury and Mars. The smaller-sized Mercury controls the nervous system, and Mars is associated with blood, muscles, and bone marrow. Then comes the largest and heaviest planet, Jupiter, which controls the fat in the human body.

Then there is hair on the head and tiny, fine hairs all over the body. Nails are on the outer part of the fingers.

Saturn, the outermost and slowest-moving planet, controls our hair and nails. It is not known when the hair and nails grow, but they do grow. The entire human body is controlled by these planets, and they affect us directly.

A horoscope is a snapshot of the sky when a person is born; the zodiac signs that rise and set at the time, and the planetary positions in them, guide the life path of the person.

Sri Aurobindo writes, "It is not always the sign of birth, however, that is most powerful in fixing the temperament, it is sometimes the sign in which the sun or the moon or else the lord of the horoscope is situated; and none of these signs can be neglected. If they are all taken into consideration according to their respective force in the horoscope, a correct idea of the character may be formed; but even then, the position and mutual relations of their lords must be taken into the account. This is the reason why men born under the same sign vary so much in character."

Sri Aurobindo further writes, "I must, however, guard against the idea that the signs and planets determine a man's character or fate. They do not, they only indicate it, because they are the sensational, celestial and astral influences or nervous force in Nature which become the instruments of our Karma. That is why the European mystics gave the name of astral planes to the plane of sensational or nervous existence and astral fluid to the magnetic power or current of nervous vital force in a man. It is this same vital force which pours upon us from all parts of the solar system and of this physical universe. But man is mightier than his sensations or vitality or the sensational or vital forces of the universe. Our fate and our temperament have been built by our own wills and our own wills can alter them." (Sri Aurobindo - The Hour of God- Premises of Astrology - Chapter II)

Ancient Hindu scriptures say that the whole universe is an expansion of the One. The idea of the creation of the universe was elaborated in the Upanishads.

Mundaka Upanishad says:

यथोर्णनाभिः सृजते गृह्णते च यथा पृथिव्यामोषधयः संभवन्ति ।
यथा सतः पुरुषात्केशलोमानि तथाऽक्षरात्संभवतीह विश्वम् ।।1.1.7।।

Yathornanabhih srijate grihnate cha,

Yatha prithivyamoshadhayah sambhavanti |

Yatha satah purushatkeshalomani,

Tatha'ksharasambhavatiha visvam ||

Translation: As the spider creates and absorbs, as medicinal plants grow from the earth, as hairs grow from the living person, so this universe proceeds from the immortal.

Chapter 3

Sun: Symbol of the Soul

The Sun represents our soul, and the position of the Sun in the zodiac signifies the karma that the soul accumulated in its previous birth. The position of the Sun indicates the inherent desire of the soul as the soul finds the most suitable zodiac sign to live in this birth, according to the karma done in the previous birth. Sun gets directional strength in the 10th house; it is considered strong here, and it helps in career advancement. Sun gets directional weakness in the 4th house, but its aspect on the 10th house makes the person wealthy and prosperous in life. The 10th house represents the social status of the person, and a strong 10th house means that the native enjoys a strong professional career in life.

The position of the Sun in the horoscope depends on the deeds of the previous life, and if the Sun is placed in the angular or trine houses, it indicates that the native has done good deeds in their previous life. Whereas, if the Sun is placed in the evil or trik houses (6th, 8th, and 12th), it indicates that the native has done bad deeds in his previous life. In due course, the person will have to reap the fruits of those bad deeds in this life.

A strong Sun represents a charismatic personality. It makes the individual determined and decisive. It bestows high energy, impressive leadership abilities, respect for elders, and good listening ability. Such a person is ambitious, energetic, influential, and compassionate. They dare to walk alone, even in difficult situations, without fear. They are unwilling to compromise on anything for their dignity and honor.

Every action done by a person affects their soul. Therefore, we should respect the dignity of every soul and never do any negative act that hurts anyone because every soul is connected to God. Expansion is the inherent desire of every soul, so we should always do such acts that expand the soul.

Any work that causes trouble to others is not the way to expansion. Every act of contraction shrinks our soul, and the person slowly starts losing their courage to walk alone. Every human being has to walk alone on the path of God, so if a person's Sun is afflicted, then he cannot be a courageous person.

3.1 Sun in Elements

3.1.1 In Fire Signs

The three fire signs are: Aries, Leo, and Sagittarius

The Sun is a fiery planet that feels extremely comfortable in the fire signs. Fire always moves upward, so the Sun in a fire sign indicates an ambitious and courageous person who never looks back. The fire sign represents inspiration, passion, warmth, idealism, and impatience.

All three fire signs are masculine signs, and a masculine planet in a masculine sign creates high energy with aggression. Fire indicates action, initiation, and appetite. Fire creates isolation, and the dominance of the fire sign displays the above-mentioned qualities of fire in a person, and such a person does not like to mix with other people.

Fire is used for creation, but it also burns, so it needs to be handled with utmost care. Fire requires fuel and has the power to radically transform things. It indicates drive for achievement and a desire to bring about radical changes. Therefore, these people take an interest in creative activities, and when the fuel is high, their energy is also high.

Fire attracts attention as well as creates fear. The Sun in fire signs indicates that these people attract attention with their presence and work, but always maintain distance from others. They are willing to help others, but they are not social or friendly people. They are not very active on social media platforms, and they rarely comment. The Sun in fire signs creates aloofness, and also from social media platforms.

The fire sign is suitable for aggressive jobs and where initiation is important. These individuals are best suited for careers in fields such as entrepreneurship, leadership, creativity, motivational speaking, education, research, and consulting–but not for jobs involving negotiation, sales and marketing.

3.1.2 In Earth Signs

The three earth signs are: Taurus, Virgo, and Capricorn.

Earth means solid base. When something is related to earth, then it is grounded and structured. It shows a person with a stable mind who always believes in a practical approach and prefers facts and figures before making a decision. Such people avoid taking unnecessary risks and prefer to secure things first.

Earth provides prosperity, but hard work is required to produce. Therefore, the earth sign indicates a very hard-working person who moves forward step by step and is never in a hurry. They know how to utilize the available resources to achieve maximum output.

Sun represents movement, and Earth represents stability. The Sun in the earth signs indicates that the person uses their energy for creative purposes. It indicates a very responsible and dedicated person who carries out responsibilities without failure.

Earth energy is a feminine and receptive energy, while the Sun is a masculine planet. The Sun being in the earth sign means that the person's aggression is reduced, and he is of a polite nature. It also indicates a slow pace with quality of patience. Earth belongs to material things; so, they want to enjoy a luxurious life and work hard to achieve it.

They perform better in organized and practical careers that yield tangible results, require diligent effort, and offer long-term financial or professional stability. Earth signs are suitable for responsible jobs; they are strong supporters and can give good suggestions, but are unable to take the initiative.

3.1.3 In Air Signs

The three air signs are: Gemini, Libra, and Aquarius.

Air is a dynamic element; it indicates an active personality who is involved in many intellectual activities. Air does not stay in one place; it indicates liberation and freedom. If air stops at one place, it starts rotting, and the flowing air always gives a feeling of freshness. The position of the Sun in the air signs shows that they are intellectual people and prefer innovative ideas in life. They get bored easily with monotonous things; they like change and are always looking for something new and exciting in life. It is very difficult for these kinds of people to do the same kind of work at the same place for their whole life.

If the total weightage of air element is high in the horoscope, then such people do not stick to one principle; they change things rapidly, and every change makes them feel like fresh air in life. It also indicates a fickle-minded person who lacks the quality of patience and wants to see the result of his efforts in a short period of time.

When there is a delay in getting the results of their work, they get nervous and leave the work midway. They own the latest gadgets that can get things done more easily and faster, and look for shortcuts in life. They want to stay updated with all the information, so they use high-quality gadgets and are good at networking.

They give priority to movement, and like the air spreads and changes its place very quickly, they quickly make their identity with their work, but it is difficult for them to stay in one place for a long time.

Air signs are good for intellectual work, but they are not responsible people and lack stability. Air indicates desire; if the desire for completion of work is over, then they immediately leave it. They excel in professions that require rapid problem-solving and creative brainstorming. They are particularly successful in fields such as networking, media and journalism, human resources, sales and marketing, and social activism.

3.1.4 In Water Signs

The three water signs are: Cancer, Scorpio, and Pisces.

Water is essential for life; its basic quality is to clean things and make things pure. The Sun in water signs indicates a nurturing quality of the person. Water is very sensitive; hence, they are sensitive people and have a strong gut feeling. They are very emotional person and quickly catch the change in feelings. It is difficult to hide the feelings and intentions from these people; they immediately sense a person's hidden objective. They like to help others and take an interest in charitable activities.

They believe in building strong bonds, but they are mysterious people who do not open up easily and hide their thoughts and feelings. Safety is always important for them, because water needs a vessel. They check the safety first and foremost. When it comes to buying something like a house or a car, they always give priority to maximum safety features; therefore, they always prefer to buy a top model car. They check the safety and comfort of a place or chair before sitting on it. They like to keep themselves safe and avoid taking unnecessary risks.

Water indicates depth in personality; they are keen observers, and nothing escapes their notice. Due to the fluid quality of water, it also indicates a very moody person. Water has the quality of freshness; they take care of every member of the family and prefer light jokes in their discussions to make the atmosphere pleasant.

Water signs are good for nurturing; their memory is sharp and remembers events after many years, but they are not aggressive person and always hesitate to take the initiative. Their innate nature helps them connect with the people around them. They thrive in roles where they can care for others, conduct in-depth research, work in the fields of healthcare or counseling–or any role that involves helping others.

While analyzing a horoscope, the right balance of all the four elements is essential; only then it reflects a person with a balanced mind.

Chapter 4

Conjunction with the Sun

Sun is the king and his conjunction with other planets is like a king sitting in his court with his various ministers. In the presence of the king, no minister is allowed to take independent decisions and only the king has the power to give orders. This does not mean that ministers have lost their presence and cannot do anything. The only thing is that they cannot give any order but they can give their valuable advice to the king and later the king can convert that advice into order. But in the presence of the king no minister can show his independent presence.

Before understanding the conjunction of other planets with the Sun, it is necessary to understand at what degree distance that planet is from the Sun and if it is close to the Sun then it is considered combust in astrology. It does not mean that all its power has been lost, rather it means that in the presence of the Sun it does not have the power to take decisions but it can advise the Sun. The combust planet shows that the Sun is not alone responsible for all the matters related to that house, but the advice of other planets also influences the decision taken by the Sun.

The planet which will be together at equal degrees near the Sun, that planet will be considered to be completely combust. The planet which is at a distance of 8 degrees from the Sun will be considered as half-combust and the planet which is at a distance of 15 degrees from the Sun will be considered as fully rising. (*Note-There are other opinions about these degrees but I consider the above degrees only.*)

When the king is absent each minister has full power to take his own decisions. Similarly, when a planet is located at a distance of more than 15 degrees from the Sun, it independently influences the matters related to that house. There may be two or more planets deciding on matters related to that house, so their relationship with each other is very important.

If the relationship is friendly then both works together and the affairs of that house prosper, if they are neutral then they do not interfere in each other's work, if they are enemies then both try to dominate each other. It indicates chaotic situations in life and matters related to that house always trouble the native. There is a lack of harmony and peace in that house and no work is done smoothly. Such a person has to work very hard to make things fruitful and when he sees some stability, unrest comes again.

4.1 Sun - Moon

The Sun represents the masculine energy and the Moon represents the feminine energy of the universe. Both these energies are constantly working and cooperating with each other for the proper functioning of universal activities. The day is ruled by the Sun and at that time the masculine energy is powerful and the night is ruled by the Moon and at that time the feminine energy is powerful. The energy during the day supports action and aggression and the energy at night supports love and compassion.

Therefore, the Moon is powerful when it is away from the Sun, because when the Sun enters the Moon disappears. When the Moon is exactly opposite the Sun (at 180°) then it is a full moon day and the Moon is at full power, it can display its light to its full potential. The Moon is considered weak within 72 degrees of the Sun. Amavasya (New Moon) occurs when both the Sun and the Moon are in the same house and less than 13.2 degrees apart from each other.

The Moon represents our mind, and when the Moon is weak in the horoscope, it indicates a lack of mental strength. It does not mean stupidity but it means that the mind is unable to face difficult situations in life. Such people get nervous easily, are always in dilemma and are unable to take decisive decisions. They say something, soon their mood changes and they say something else. Moon near the Sun indicates a person with an unstable mind. They are very emotional people, always looking for security around them and incapable of taking risks in life.

Due to the brightness of the Sun, the Moon becomes unable to show its presence in front of the Sun. In other words, she can't stand the heat of the Sun. The legend related to Sun and his wife states that his wife left him because she could not bear the heat of the Sun. Planets too close to the Sun lose their independence but the Moon disappears completely.

This combination indicates a polite person who stays away from mischievous activities. They are mild-mannered, happy-go-lucky people with no ulterior motives. However, they are easily influenced by the outside environment be it change in weather or conditions. Their immune system is weak and they fall ill easily. Moon also represents mother, so these people should always have a good relationship with their mother or motherly figure and should always serve them to strengthen their Moon.

4.2 Sun - Mars

We can understand the conjunction of Sun and Mars as if a king is standing with his generals. Both are masculine, aggressive and friendly planets. When a king stands with his generals, his power becomes immense, therefore, Sun is exalted in Aries which is sign of Mars. This energy makes a person confident, courageous and determined. The king stands with his generals and discusses the state of the kingdom and gives orders for action. Therefore, the people with this type of conjunction have very active and aggressive personalities. This high energy does not let them sit still and they work hard to get the results of their work.

When energy of both the planets supports each other then it enhances the matter related to that house. It indicates a strong will and daring attitude of the person and they belong to army, police or other jobs where high energy is required.

They are ambitious person and desire to achieve power and authority in their life. They are impulsive, take decisions on the fly, and never shy away from taking initiative. Therefore, they are never afraid to face adverse situations in life. They are stubborn, do not listen to others' suggestions and always put their own decisions above all else.

When energy is in excess then it needs to be given proper direction; They perform better in athletics and other sports where correct channelization of high energy is required. Improper use of energy creates anger and destruction. They are ready for conflict at any time and fight fiercely. They take big risks and are never afraid of any opponent. This combination creates a combative personality and they want to win every challenge. They are not afraid to venture into unknown territory and they enjoy the thrill of the chase. They cannot sit still even when they do not have any clear direction in life. Due to excess energy they try in wrong direction and waste energy.

When energy is high it must always be in good hands otherwise disaster is possible. Therefore, to give proper direction to such energy a strong a well-placed Jupiter is required to show the way to the correct utilization of such energy.

4.3 Sun - Mercury

Sun is known as the father and Mercury is the prince who represents a young child. Wherever the child goes, his father is aware of his activities. In astrology Mercury cannot move more than 28 degrees away from the Sun and the Sun-Mercury conjunction is known as "Budhaditya Yoga".

Mercury is known as the messenger and significator of all types of communication. Many astrologers believe that Mercury never combust and I also believe in the same. A child's demands can influence a father's decision and the father cannot ignore them. In the same way, the decision of the Sun is influenced by the Mercury on the matters related to the house. This planet, which controls every type of communication, has full power to influence the decision taken by the Sun (soul).

Therefore, while analyzing this conjunction, it is necessary to analyze Mercury independently. Strong Mercury indicates a good grip in terms of communication while weak Mercury indicates problems. When Mercury is behind the Sun it indicates impulsive behavior and fast communication because when the child is behind the father he wants to come to the father quickly. When the father is behind the child, the child feels relaxed and plays with a calm mind and without any worries. When the Sun is behind Mercury the person deals with all matters related to communication calmly and avoids being hasty.

According to astrology, when the planets come near the Sun, their speed becomes very fast and when they move away from the Sun, their speed slows down. Therefore, Saturn, the most distant planet, teaches us patience because its speed is very slow.

Mercury represents the intelligence of a person. Strong Mercury indicates logical thinking and mathematical ability to the person. A child should grow up with his/ her parents, without any proper guidance a child can easily get influenced by the mischievous people of the society. If Mercury is alone in the horoscope and is under influence of malefic planets, then such a person uses his intelligence only in negative activities.

4.4 Sun - Jupiter

Jupiter is the planet of healing. If a person takes proper medication, diet, and cares for their wounds, healing is good and fast. This doesn't mean you should just leave it at that and wait for a miracle to change everything overnight. The healing provided by Jupiter doesn't always mean medical treatment, but rather bringing positive changes in life in terms of hope, rewards, growth, and prosperity. However, people view astrology in the wrong way. Instead of working hard towards their goals, they expect a miracle to happen and all their problems to be solved overnight. Therefore, cheap remedies easily attract people.

Jupiter takes about a year to cross a sign and complete the entire zodiac in 12 years. Therefore, after every 12 years, Jupiter transits over its natal Jupiter, and that time brings remarkable changes in the life of the person. Jupiter is the most benefic planet, so its transit brings luck, happiness, and success in life. When Jupiter transits over the natal Moon or the 7th house or its lord or makes an aspect, then most of the native's marriages happen at that time. It bestows the person with children, wealth, and a happy life.

Jupiter is a teacher. Just as when a teacher enters a classroom, all the children open their books and begin to read, and their knowledge begins to grow. Children receive necessary guidance from the teacher and begin to complete their work. Similarly, the house in which Jupiter transits begins to develop, and things begin to settle down as if the teacher has entered the classroom.

The planets in the house on which Jupiter's aspect falls receive necessary guidance and begin to complete their tasks, just as students begin to complete their work under the guidance of a teacher. Until Jupiter's aspect, a person wanders without direction. As soon as Jupiter's aspect falls, things begin to settle down. A person now has direction for what to do in life.

The transit of Jupiter affects the physical and spiritual life of the native. It depends on what you are looking for in life and how hard you have worked towards your goal. The result of the transit of Jupiter happens more like a reward; it brings the results of past efforts and preparation and contributes to growth. When Jupiter transits over the natal planets and forms an aspect with other planets, then multiple events take shape in the life of the person.

Saturn signifies the hard work done by a person, and Jupiter signifies rewards. When Jupiter transits over the natal Saturn after 12 years, the person gets rewards for their past work. The hard work done by a person never goes in vain. You may not get the reward at the time you are expecting, but the hard work of the native gets recorded in the books of Saturn. The planet of justice dispenses justice when the time comes.

Jupiter is the lord of gold, and it bestows marriage and children. It is called the planet of fortune as it governs finances and family. Jupiter transiting over the natal Sun or aspecting the natal Sun creates fortunate moments in life. In the 12-year cycle of Jupiter, the conjunction and aspect of Jupiter with the natal Sun provide opportunities for expansion and growth. During this time, the native achieves success in his endeavors. The native gets auspicious results like a new job, promotion, rise in rank, or a long journey on the excursion. During this transit, the native travels to visit important temples and performs religious rituals and Yagna.

The Sun is called the soul, and Jupiter is called the Jiva (body). The conjunction of Jupiter with the natal Sun is a time of a combination of expansive energy and self-awareness. This conjunction shows a vibrant personality who can make necessary and correct decisions. This is an excellent time to start new ventures and explore new areas. This energy supports learning, so it is a good time to start learning a new subject and expand your horizons.

When Jupiter conjuncts or aspects the natal Sun, this is the time when the native's twelve years of hard work bear fruit. During this period, the native gains fame, respect, and admiration for their work. They receive the support of noble and respected figures. The native's father receives the rewards of his hard work. On the other hand, if the Sun is not auspicious in the birth chart, the possibility of over-enthusiasm, dominance, and arrogance cannot be ruled out.

When the energy supports expansion and growth, this is the time to embrace diversity and develop relationships that enrich understanding about various new aspects of life. The Sun-Jupiter conjunction or aspect means that one should be prepared for such expansion, as it is the time to take advantage of the opportunity. One should take the initiative to utilize it in a more creative way to promote auspicious things in life.

This is an excellent time to set long-term goals, as this energy helps set the right direction in life. This transit provides a clear vision for making decisions related to financial investments. Therefore, it's time to identify your core strengths and move forward with your goals. When favorable winds begin to blow in your life, you can feel confident in your decisions. This is a time to reap the benefits of your efforts. If you've worked hard and don't hold any ill will toward anyone, a firm decision made at this time will reward you.

4.5 Sun - Venus

According to astrology, the relationship between Sun and Venus is inimical. Venus is said to be the lord of arts and represents feminine qualities. While King Sun is a masculine and krura (fierce) planet. Venus is the hottest planet due to the presence of carbon dioxide, clouds and acid, while Mercury is the planet closest to the Sun.

Despite being the hottest planet, Venus has gentle qualities and is considered the goddess of love. Love is very delicate, it has tenderness and cannot be treated strictly. Love is like a fresh flower and it withers as soon as it hardens. Just like we have to hold a fresh flower with delicate hands, love also requires the same delicacy. Sun is bold and forceful having no soft qualities and there is no place for tender feelings near it. Ruling a kingdom requires taking tough decisions and toughness is exactly the opposite of Venus's nature. Therefore, these are two different energies where the symmetry is completely missing. Hence, a person having this conjunction has to face tough situations in life.

Venus wants art, music and love and Sun is devoid of all these qualities. People with this conjunction tend to have the qualities of Venus but they have to face difficult situations in life where their soft qualities do not take shape because all these qualities are absent in the Sun. Hence, their efforts go in vain.

Sun is the hot planet which represents action and dryness and Venus is the soft planet which represents politeness and freshness. Venus is the ruler of fresh water, a very close combination indicates that water evaporates and dryness remains. Therefore, Venus feels uncomfortable in displaying its qualities and becomes suppressed if it is combusted. When Venus passes over the Sun in transit it indicates that all the water on Venus has dried up. Water indicates not only emotions but also relationships and bonds. A close conjunction between Sun and Venus indicates relationship is dried.

This conjunction indicates that Venus's softness gradually begins to dry up in various circumstances of their lives. If the conjunction falls in the 7th house, the person with this combination has tender qualities but he may face tough behavior from his partner whose reactions may dry his tender tendencies. Whenever they want softness in life, they always get a harsh answer. Slowly, the flower of tenderness starts withering from their lives.

Venus wants to enjoy the joys and luxuries of life but Sun is always busy with matters of state (work) and does not have time for all these activities. It shows that the person wants to enjoy luxuries but circumstances do not support him. Gradually, the tender feelings of Venus begin to dry up. Venus always avoids quarrel and turmoil at any cost, and tries to lead a happy and peaceful life, but Sun shows arrogance and anger.

The qualities of these two planets are totally differed from each other. A person with this conjunction wants to live a peaceful life which he does not get. Sun is extremely fierce planet and Venus is extremely soft planet, due to the difference in the basic nature of both, the combination of both spoils the matter of that house. No matter how many differences exist between these two planets, Venus does not go beyond 48 degrees from the Sun.

Therefore, before doing any analysis it is necessary to check the distance between these two planets. If the distance between the Sun and Venus is more than 43 degrees and 20 minutes then it indicates delay in marriage. A very close conjunction to Sun and Venus also causes eye problems. I have seen in my experience that a person gets glasses late in life whose difference between Sun and Venus is more than 28 degrees. If this difference is less than 5 degrees then vision weakens quickly. Venus represents transparent glasses then he has to take help of glasses. A person with weak Venus is unable to handle delicate glasses and often breaks them.

We can understand this combination from some more examples from life. In the presence of women, men like to show their gentle behavior to attract their attention. They stop fighting and abusing each other and wait for the woman to leave the place. The mere presence of a single woman has the power to change the heat of the discussion because no man wants to expose his absurd behavior to a woman. Similarly, the presence of Venus affects the decisions taken by the Sun. Sun cannot be always rude in presence of Venus. Hence, this combination enhances the creative qualities of the person and makes the person soft, gentle and humble.

These people are interested in love, art, music, fashion and like to eat rich and tasty food. Venus is a very sophisticated planet which shows that gentle behavior, manners and etiquette are their top priority and this conjunction indicates a person with such qualities. But these people have to face dryness in love related matters because a close conjunction indicates that the water of Venus evaporates. However, a close conjunction to Sun is good for spirituality. When Venus is far from Sun it indicates more water that means an emotional person. Such a person is good at building relationships and maintains strong bonds with his friends and family. They are not ready to leave those people to whom they love.

Their negative side is that they are very emotional, even small things hurt them. They spend more than their capacity and show off unnecessarily.

4.6 Sun - Saturn

Sun is the soul which represents light and Saturn is the main ruler of death and represents darkness. These are two opposite energies. According to astrology, the relationship between Sun and Saturn is inimical. When planets with opposite energies meet in any house of the horoscope then they do not support each other and start dominating to show their supremacy and this creates disturbance in the matter of that house. For example, Sun is the indicator of time and Saturn is the indicator of the end of time.

Hence, this combination shows that the watch of such a person will never work properly, either he will lose it or it will get damaged. The poor watch has been gone in the fight between Sun and Saturn. There is another meaning of this conjunction. Damage of watch indicates damage of time, the Sun-Saturn conjunction indicates a delay in time. Therefore, there is a delay in things happening and nothing happens on time in their lives.

Following are some more differences for better understanding of these two energies;

1. Sun is a fiery planet, due to its influence things become hot, active and agile. Saturn is a cold planet, due to its influence things become freeze and isolated, speed slows down and every activity stops.
2. Sun is the king and Saturn is the guard. When the king arrives, the doors are opened and the guard's

job is to close and lock the doors. When the Sun comes in the morning the darkness goes away, when the Sun goes in the evening the darkness returns. These two are opposite functions and both cannot happen simultaneously.

3. Sun is the beginning of activity and Saturn brings limits, restrictions and takes things to their end; Saturn is "The End".
4. Sun represents autocracy and Saturn represents democracy.
5. Sun shows ego and Saturn brings down every ego. Saturn shows the real truth of life and makes the person humble by removing all types of ego.

Hence, this combination indicates overcoming ego because Saturn means being devoid of ego. Saturn creates many obstacles to reduce the ego, this shows that the more ego a person has, the more obstacles he will have to face in his life. Saturn is an emotionless planet which teaches discipline and hard work in life. This combination makes the person extremely practical who stays away from all kinds of gossip and manipulation.

Rahu work as an agent to Saturn and has full power to engulf the Sun i.e., remove light in the life of the person. Therefore, giving up ego and becoming a humble person is the only key to overcome the negative effects of this conjunction. If this conjunction occurs in Aries then it indicates a high ego whereas if it occurs in Libra then it indicates a humble person.

Sun represents father and authority and Saturn who is his son represents masses and working-class people.

Saturn is the planet of justice and brings balance. The judge shows no mercy while giving justice. That is why Saturn shows no mercy to the Sun and destroys all its negativity. This combination indicates that the person will not have a cordial relationship with his bosses and will challenge his superiors for any wrong doing. It indicates wild arguments between father or authority figure and in transit the situation become worst. Therefore, the career of these individuals is inconsistent as both Sun and Saturn are the karakas of the tenth house which is the house of career and the fight between these two, spoils the career like a watch gone haywire in the above example.

In the house in which this conjunction occurs, the person has to face various obstacles. For example, if this conjunction falls in the fifth house then the person faces problems in his creativity and the child is our creation. Hence, such a person has to face problems in marital life or children related problems.

If this combination comes in the fourth or tenth house in the horoscope of a native, then it is not good for his professional life. He has to face a lot of struggle to make his way. The aspect of these two planets with each other in the fourth and tenth houses also creates a lot of struggle in the native's professional life and he gets initial success in his career after a lot of struggle. The maturity age of Sun is 22 years and the maturity age of Saturn is 36 years. Hence, the life of such a person between the age of 22 to 36 years is full of struggle.

The Positive Thing

The positive thing is that this combination gives birth to a very mature person. However, many kinds of obstacles come in their life but they are always ready to fight them. They tend to be self-made individuals and achieve success through their own efforts, although their learning curve may be longer than others. They become down to earth people and are ready to remove every obstacle from his life. They remain isolated from others, become spiritual and take interest in occult. On the higher aspect, this combination indicates that the person will seek the light but will have to go on the path of darkness and one cannot move towards the light without seeing the real truth of life where the biggest obstacle is one's ego.

On the Downside

The downside is that they become undisciplined and pessimistic individuals who lack goals in life. Instead of becoming humble, they become timid, avoid challenges and do not have the courage to face adversities.

4.7 Sun - Rahu

Both Sun and Rahu are enemies of each other. Sun is the king of light and Rahu is the king of illusion and darkness. When light comes, darkness automatically goes away. There are two types of darkness, the first is that in which a person knows that he is in darkness. One who is aware about his darkness seeks light, Saturn represents that darkness. As such, the seeker of truth knows that he is in darkness and he keeps wandering here and there in search of light. The second is that darkness which a person does not even realize that he is in darkness. He believes only in snatching and looting things from others like, fraudsters, hackers, thieves, robbers etc. They have no realization that they are living in darkness, that darkness is ruled by Rahu.

When Sun rises in the morning, the darkness of the night automatically disappears. In fact, it disappears even before the Sun comes over the horizon. So, Rahu cannot be present where Sun is present but the voice of the soul (Sun) can be suppressed by material desires (Rahu) and giving priority to material desires is to strengthen Rahu.

Rahu is a disturbed energy, in which house it presents it creates disturbances. The close association of a planet with Rahu indicates that planet always get disturbed and that bring many ups and downs in life. One should never try for shortcuts to get success in life, because it disappears soon, anything given by Rahu disappears quickly, Rahu is never reliable.

On the day of the eclipse, Rahu has the full power to swallow the Sun, which shows that one can push back one's soul to satisfy one's material desires. But the soul is immortal and Rahu cannot defeat it. Therefore, during an eclipse, the Sun disappears from the sky only for a short period of time. Following are some more differences between these two energies;

1. Sun represents sattva while Rahu is a master of sin.

2. Sun is the giver while Rahu has no intention to give anything, it is always taker.

3. Sun is the king and makes rules while Rahu is rebellious and enjoy to break the rules.
4. Sun follow the righteous path while Rahu always take interest in mischievous paths and shortcuts to achieve the desire.
5. Sun is forthright while Rahu is conspiratorial.

The combination of Sun and Rahu in astrology in known as grahan dosh. When the two opposite energies meet at one place, the life of the person is not a smooth life. It gives birth to many difficulties and the person has to face a lot of struggle in his life. It indicates difficulty to father and when Rahu transit in the sign of Leo or over the Sun such difficulties arises after the age of 42 years.

To overcome the negatives of this conjunction, one should never pursue one's material desires and should always give priority to religious activities. Rahu movement is opposite to that of other planets i.e., he does not like to follow traditional paths, thinks in the opposite language and likes to go against the order. But Rahu needs the help of others to act because he does not have hands and legs, hence, he influences other planets with his thoughts.

Sun - Rahu conjunction means that the energy of the Sun is influenced by Rahu. Hence, the thinking and actions of such a person are different from others. This combination shows that the person will not support old and conservative ideas and will bring changes in the system. He will put forth new and revolutionary ideas which may not be accepted by the traditional followers but he can never support conventions of the society.

Therefore, this combination gives birth to rebels and revolutionaries.

The downside is that malicious desire of a person can swallow the piousness of the person and he is force by his desire to follow the path of darkness. They become power hungry people and misuse their authority to fulfill his desire. They always adopt rebellious attitude towards government or father and enjoy creating trouble for others.

4.8 Sun - Ketu

Ketu - The South Node of the Moon, known as the planet of separation which means end of all attachment. When one thing is separated from another it destroys all types of communication and relationships. The person is not interested in meeting people, going for parties; hence, Ketu represents silence. Ketu is a fiery planet and the place where it has influence starts drying up and becomes barren. It is a mysterious planet and gives birth to unexpected events in life.

Rahu means running after desire and Ketu means that the person has the experience of running after desire. Ketu indicates that the person does not take any interest in the matters related to that house as he has no attachment to it.

For example, when Ketu is placed in the tenth house the person has no attachment to his workplace. He is doing his work because he has to, but when the time is up he does not like to sit in the office even for a minute more. While Rahu in the tenth house shows a desirous and workaholic person who sit for long hours.

Ketu indicates victory, but every victory requires hard work and sacrifices. Ketu has no attachment, it indicates that the person does not hesitate to sacrifice those things to achieve success where Ketu is placed. For example, Ketu in the 4th house indicates that the person stays most of the time out of his home and do sacrifices related with the 4th house to achieve purpose of his life.

Ketu has no head, it represents hidden things and the ability to penetrate. Ketu is not interested in show-off activities, it provides energy to the person to go deeper and find hidden truths. That is why these people are very good at researching and finding secrets and the biggest mystery is the "Creator" of the universe himself. The scriptures say that it is present everywhere but we cannot see it with these physical eyes.

This shows that there is some power in the body of every human being whose development makes the person enlightened and as that capacity increases, the person becomes capable of knowing the invisible and in common parlance it is called intuition. Therefore, Ketu is the planet of intuition, spirituality and enlightenment. Enlightenment cannot be seen with these physical eyes; therefore, Ketu has no aspects.

This combination shows that the person takes interest in spirituality and stays away from unnecessary wandering in worldly affairs. Ketu cuts off every negative influence of the Sun present inside the person and makes the person a seeker of truth. Ketu brings many changes in life and forces the person to follow the path which is his true purpose. Therefore, Ketu can influence the Sun partially, but not completely, hence, the Sun-Ketu conjunction forms a partial solar eclipse.

These people find success in fields that require the ability to uncover hidden secrets. They are proficient in astrology, palmistry and other secret sciences and dive into the ocean of spirituality after the age of 49.

Sun and Ketu both are fiery planets and Ketu indicates explosion. It indicates excessive heat in the house where this conjunction occurs and if it occurs in a fiery sign the situation can be dire. If the person does not channel such energy into spirituality then it can cause great harm.

The negative side is that they lack patience, are indecisive and get restless easily. They lack self-confidence, go into depression and isolate themselves from others. Instead of finding positive activities they take interest in negative activities and while doing so they are able to hide their real face from others because Ketu has no face.

Chapter 5

Moon: The Significator of the Mind

In astrology, the Moon and Venus represent two forms of feminine energy. The Moon symbolizes receptivity, intuition, and maternal energy. Venus symbolizes tenderness, aesthetic beauty, and love. The Moon is considered the significator of the mind and emotions. Its various waxing and waning phases are like the ups and downs of human emotions, and therefore, it is considered a significator of the mind. Its nakshatra reflects a person's inherent human nature, and its transit with various natal planets gives rise to possible results.

It is a watery planet, representing moist and rainy season and watery places like well, water tanks, bathrooms, watery surfaces, rivers, bays, ocean, etc. Its color is white and indicates a small height. It represents new fabric and organic matter. It represents salty taste (sea salt, rock salt), gems, spotless pearls, silver, and other white metals. It belongs to the Vaishya caste and represents the age of 70 years old. It represents the coconut tree, fruits, vegetables, and all watery substances.

The Moon is the only natural satellite of the Earth. Its average distance from Earth is 385,000 km, and the Earth rotates on its axis once every 27.3 days (a sidereal month). Its daytime temperature is 225°F (107°C), while night-time temperatures are -243°F (-153°C). It has a solid, rocky surface covered with craters, mountain ranges, rills (long narrow channels), and lava plains.

5.1.1 Direction and Digbala

The direction of the Moon is North-West; it gets directional strength (Digbala) in the 4th house and weakness in the 10th house.

5.1.2 Synodic and Sidereal Period of the Moon

It moves 13.2 degrees per day, completes one orbit around the Earth in 27.3 days, and rises on average 50 minutes late every day. The half of the Moon that is towards the Sun can be seen from the Earth and is called the phases of the Moon. The cycle of lunar phases takes 29.5 days, known as the synodic period, which is longer than the sidereal period of 27.3 days. The reason for this difference is that the Moon returns to the same place in the sky once every sidereal period, but the Sun is also moving in the sky. When the Moon returns to the same place in the sky, the Sun moves 27 degrees. It takes the Moon about two days to catch this difference.

Understanding the different phases of the Moon is very important in astrology. When the Moon is exactly opposite the Sun (180° or 7th house) in a horoscope, it is a full moon day. The Moon is considered weak within 72 degrees from the Sun. Amavasya (new moon) occurs when the Sun and Moon are both in the same house and less than 13.2 degrees from each other.

5.2 Moon Controls Our Minds

The Moon is a Sattvik planet and controls our minds. It is a feminine planet that represents the mother in the chart, peace of mind, and rules our emotions. It represents selflessness like a mother and the tender qualities of a female. It represents the nourishing quality, sensitivity, and imagination of the person. A strong Moon indicates a strong mind, a friendly nature, and a pleasing personality. The person is receptive, decisive, mature, helpful in nature, and clear in thoughts. A strong Moon fosters a personality that understands and respects the feelings of others. Such individuals possess a stable mind and can remain calm even in stressful situations. Such a person never wastes time on trivialities; they want to get straight to the point and have no interest in idle chatter.

5.3 Moon - The Significator of Relationships

The Moon is a significator of emotions and relationships. Its position determines how strong we feel within ourselves. It also reflects our relationships with others and how we connect to them. A strong Moon in the horoscope indicates a strong mind, while a weak Moon indicates a fickle mind, frequent mood swings, dependency, and instability.

The Moon represents;

Family: It represents nurturing and emotional care within a family.

Home Life: It represents domestic life, home environment, personal, and inner world.

Emotional bonding: Attraction, harmony, relationships, dependency, and emotional security.

Creativity: Imagination, art, music, photography, poetry, writing.

Lineage: Maternal lineage and inherited family traits.

5.4 Moon Represents Home and Mother

The Moon is associated with the home and family life. Being the representative of the mother in the horoscope, the person should always respect their mother and should never quarrel with her, if they want their Moon to always remain strong.

5.5 Moon - The Queen

Moon is considered the queen of the solar system. Its own sign is Cancer; it gets exalted in Taurus at 3 degrees, which is also its Mooltrikona sign, and debilitated in Scorpio at 3 degrees. The sign of Taurus is highly suitable for the Moon. Taurus is a feminine sign - fertile and receptive, it is a highly fertile land in the zodiac. The nature of Taurus is to produce and grow things. Its symbol is the bull, which is known for its sensuality and fertility. Taurus represents luxury and comfort;

therefore, the Moon – the Queen, finds this sign perfectly suitable for herself, and becomes exalted at 3 degrees in the sign (*Upon entering here, the queen found a very suitable place for her stay*). Scorpio is a sign of ruthlessness and represents muddy water, which is totally against the nature of the Moon – the Queen, and it gets debilitated in the sign while entering (3 degrees).

5.6 Moon in Different Signs

Taurus is ruled by Venus, and the Moon governs our mind, emotions, and sensitivities. All higher forms of genius require Venus to be strong. Taurus is a fixed sign, and the exalted Moon indicates that creativity is high when the mind is calm and stable. Therefore, when the Moon transits in Venus, the mind becomes stable, imaginative, and active. This period favors new creativity. It provides more concentration and the power to work on long-lasting things.

Mercury is the planet signifying intelligence. When the Moon transits in Mercury's sign (Gemini or Virgo), the person is mentally active and keen to explore new ideas. If other aspects are positive, the person uses his intelligence for the welfare of mankind. Negative use of intelligence is also possible, and the person uses his intelligence for destructive activities.

Mars is the planet of anger and aggression. When the Moon transits in the zodiac sign of Mars (Aries and Scorpio), quarrels and violent activities start, and people with a criminal mindset take steps to fulfill their nefarious desires. The sign of Jupiter (Sagittarius and Pisces) indicates religious activities, fantasy, and imagination. The sign of Saturn (Capricorn, Aquarius) indicates hard work and concentration.

5.7 The Moon Affect Life on Earth

The Moon profoundly influences human life. Mental health, sleep problems, menstruation, violent behavior, and many other illnesses are all linked to the Moon at one time or another. It has a profound connection with water and agriculture. Its gravitational pull causes ocean tides and affects soil moisture.

According to medical astrology, operations should not be performed during the full moon, as this time causes excess fluid to accumulate in the body. To avoid swelling and complications after surgery, surgery should also be avoided when the Moon is under any aspect of Mars. It is best to perform surgery during the Moon's waxing phases, i.e., between the new moon and the full moon.

5.8 Moon Represents Masses

Moon rules over the masses; the 4th house is the house of the masses. If the Moon is situated in the 4th house, then the popularity of the person is indicated. Moon, being a feminine planet, bestows attractiveness and other feminine qualities. The person under the influence of the Moon as a ruling planet takes an interest in taking care of others. It indicates professions related to fluids, doctors, psychologists, therapists, child care, and other nurturing and healing professions.

5.9 Moon is Associated with Travel

In astrology, because it is a fast-moving planet, it is associated with change and a love for travel. Its tendency towards rapid change awakens a natural desire within the native to travel and witness changing landscapes. Just as the Moon changes from day to day, the native - after staying in one place for a day - becomes eager to move to another the very next day. Consequently, a person with a weak Moon soothes their mind by wandering about throughout the day.

The third house signifies short journeys; therefore, the placement of the Moon in the third house or in the sign of Gemini indicates that the person will undertake many short journeys in life. That is why individuals born under the sign of Gemini make good salespeople. The ninth house signifies long journeys; thus, the placement of the Moon in the ninth house or in the sign of Sagittarius indicates that the person will undertake long-distance or foreign journeys.

5.10 The Sun and The Moon

i. The Sun represents the father, the moon represents the mother.

ii. The Sun represents the seed, the Moon represents the womb.

iii. The Sun represents the order, and the Moon represents the fulfillment of the order. The Moon has no light and is always dependent on sunlight.

This means that a person influenced by the Moon always obeys their elders and superiors.

iv. The Sun shows independence, and the weak Moon indicates that the person is looking for support and is always afraid of being alone.

v. The Sun represents the ego and the conscious mind. The Moon governs the inner and private self.

vi. The Sun symbolizes public life, career and external identity. The Moon governs the subconscious world of emotions and domestic realms.

vii. The Sun represents the present, the Moon represents the past. If Moon is situated in any house from the 9th to 12th house, then the person takes interest in subjects like; History, Archaeology, Astrology, etc. The person memorizes the dates of historical events easily and is quick to learn these subjects.

5.11 Moon - A Fickle Planet

In astrology, the Moon is often called the "fickle" planet because it is associated with a person's changing emotions and moods. It stays in each zodiac sign for approximately two and a half days. Its transit through the zodiac influences the constantly changing flow of the mind. A weak Moon indicates a weak mind. Such people find it difficult to stay in one place. They may engage in a task for a short time and then abandon it and start another, but they don't stay there for long. They frequently change the arrangement of their rooms, furniture, curtains, etc. They enjoy wandering aimlessly, but find it difficult to sit in one place. Therefore, many people feel very restless in their homes during the holidays.

5.12 Saturn and Moon

Saturn teaches stability in life; therefore, any connection of Saturn with the Moon is an indication that the wandering of such a person will stop. Therefore, when Saturn transits through the natal Moon, it puts a stop to every useless wandering. The person's life will not remain the same as before. Therefore, according to many, Sade Sati creates problems; and when it concludes, the individual is no longer the same–they are changed forever. Saturn teaches stability, and the mind learns to be stable through the difficult lessons taught by Saturn. Therefore, when Sade Sati begins, the person begins to face problems that teach them patience in life. Many people become religious, and they like to practice various techniques of meditation.

The conjunction of Saturn and the Moon is not good for seeking worldly things in life. Saturn puts limits and restrictions on worldly pleasures and tries its best to control the person's fickle state of mind. Therefore, if the Moon is weak in this conjunction, the person gets anxious very quickly. However, this conjunction is very good for a religious nature. They are philosophical, seek spiritual knowledge, sit in meditation, and lead a sattvic life.

5.13 Moon denotes Private Affairs

The Moon represents a person's inner world and private affairs. It governs our emotions, instincts, and intuition. It determines how we process and react to our experiences without any filters. It reflects what makes a person feel emotionally safe and comfortable. It governs the intimate part of the personality that is not always obvious to others. The Moon's conjunction or aspect with Jupiter leads to liberalism and openness, while its conjunction or aspect with Saturn leads to silence. Therefore, the transit or aspect of Jupiter upon the Moon brings auspiciousness to a person's life, whereas the transit of Saturn causes mental stress and brings about major life changes, including shifts in one's private affairs.

5.14 Moon represents Money & Liquid Assets

In Vedic astrology, the Moon is associated with money, daily cash flow, and liquid assets. It is associated with daily needs and nourishment. It represents flowing money rather than fixed assets. Like a waxing and waning moon, it represents money that flows in and out. It is associated with small, frequent transactions and is related to businesses such as milk and food items. It represents the key that leads to wealth, while Jupiter represents the safe (vault) and Venus represents the treasure. In financial astrology, the planets represent the following major things;

i. Sun - Career, power, authority, and leadership

ii. Moon - Money in wallet, daily cash flow, and liquidity

iii. Mars - Real estate and landed property

iv. Mercury – Intelligence, communication, speech, and business

v. Jupiter - Increase in wealth, savings, prosperity, and right direction

vi. Venus - Comfort, luxury, and vehicle

vii. Saturn - Long-lasting assets and long-term stability

viii. Rahu - Sudden success & wealth, short-term success

The Moon is associated with the mind, and the mind is closely linked to emotions and thoughts. Therefore, the person who has deep emotional bonds with others can easily give their keys to others. In the present age of technology, the key is replaced with a password. However, individuals with a weak Moon may make the mistake of sharing their passwords or keys with others while acting on impulse. Swayed by emotion, they might disclose details about money to others, leading to significant losses later on. Therefore, it is not advisable for a person with a weak Moon to share their money, passwords, or keys with others, as they might be making such decisions based on emotions–something they could come to regret later.

A strong and well-placed Moon gives peace of mind, which helps in making better and wiser financial decisions. If the Moon is weak or afflicted in a horoscope, a person may overspend due to emotions. If a person has an emotional connection with another person and if their Moon is weak or inauspicious, they may spend money or on them without thinking.

The Moon is considered weak within 72 degrees of the Sun. The direction of the Moon is North-West; it gets directional strength (Digbala) in the 4th house and weakness in the 10th house. Its exaltation sign is Taurus, debilitation sign is Scorpio, and own sign is Cancer. A weak Moon can bring down both financial and emotional matters, leading to confusion and wrong decisions.

A strong Moon helps in making smart decisions that lead to sound financial decisions. The presence of the Moon in the fourth house of the horoscope or its strong position means having liquid money, cash in the wallet, and public support because the 4th house is related to the masses. A weak Moon or Moon in the 10th house means a lack of cash in the wallet. For a good flow of cash in the wallet, connection between Moon (cash) and 11th house (gains) or 2nd house (savings) is considered very good. An afflicted Moon in the 12th house means that the native may suffer loss of wallet sometime in his life.

Jupiter is considered the most auspicious planet in astrology, and it is related to wealth expansion. Therefore, Jupiter's aspect on the Moon or its connection with the Moon in the birth chart or transit is very auspicious for strengthening the cash flow in the wallet.

5.15 Weak Moon and Remedies

When the Moon is placed less than 72 degrees from the Sun, it indicates less sunlight, and due to the absence of sunlight, the native is prone to diseases easily. A weak Moon indicates emotional instability, overreact to situations and confusion in making decisions. Its weakness often manifests as anxiety, mood swings, poor sleep, and lack of mental clarity.

Key Signs of a Weak Moon

i. A weak or afflicted moon indicates a person will become depressed, pessimistic, impulsive, timid, self-destructive, insane, and psychic.

ii. It leads to issues such as incessant talking, over-anxious, and frequent restlessness.

iii. A weak Moon implies that a person can be easily influenced by external energies and struggles to make firm decisions.

iv. It leads to mental fatigue and sleep disturbances.

v. It causes difficulties in relationships and creates tension in the bond with one's mother or a mother-figure.

vi. A weak Moon can lead to water-related issues or hormonal imbalances.

Remedies:

1. Read good books

2. Worship Lord Shiva

2. Observe the Monday fast

3. The negative influence of the Moon can be mitigated by caring for one's mother or any other elderly woman.

4. Meditate for a few minutes every morning.

5. Immediately stop any water leaks in your home.

6. Stop sharing information about one person with another.

7. Never share secrets with anyone.

8. Never waste food or water. Feed extra food to animals or birds.

9. Wear pearls and silver.

10. One should stay away from any kind of dispute.

11. Avoid watching frivolous serials on mobile phones and television. Turn off the television, computer, mobile, etc., at least one hour before going to sleep.

12. Chant Mantra – "Om Somaya Namah" or "Om Shraam Shreem Shraum Sah Chandramase Namah". These mantras should be chanted 108 times on Monday or at the time of moonrise.

Chapter 6

Mars: The Push Energy

The Red Planet, Mars, is considered the Commander-in-Chief of the Solar System and denotes strength. Named after the Roman god of war, this planet symbolizes action, drive, and desire. The energy of Mars inspires us to recognize when and where we need to move forward in life by adopting a warrior-like spirit, and where we should not give up our efforts; instead, we should keep trying continuously.

It is considered a tamasic and fiery planet. It is a masculine and Kshatriya (warrior) caste planet. It is a dry and barren planet, and indicates a tense and quarrelsome situation. It represents accidents, fires, disputes, destruction, war, and sexual drive. Its color is blood-red, and the stone is coral. It represents the summer season and fiery places. It deals with burnt clothing and inorganic substances. It represents a young age and low height. Its metal is iron, taste is bitter, and tendency is violent. It represents upward movement.

The energy of Mars is a driving force that compels ambition, passion, and desire to move forward and achieve fulfillment. It is a direct and clear energy, essential for initiating any endeavor. It helps in facing challenges, putting up a strong fight, and achieving victory with courage and a competitive spirit, despite difficult circumstances. It determines the approach to achieving the goal—whether it is a bold initiative (Fire sign), unwavering patience (Earth sign), a well-thought-out strategy (Air sign), or a natural flow (Water sign).

The energy of Mars means;

- No hesitation
- No regrets
- Proactive
- Learning from trials and errors
- Overcome obstacles

Mars represents the masculine aspect of dynamic energy, governing both creation and destruction through the application of force and driving one to complete tasks even in difficult circumstances. The energy of Mars works to turn adverse circumstances in one's favor by using hard work and force. It is the energy of Mars that forces the person to move forward, remove fear and accept challenges. Strong Mars shows bravery and strength to face any difficult situation. The energy of Mars cannot be contained. It is essential to channel this energy outward, and this is typically done through work, hard labor, and other physical activities.

It emphasizes working hard to fulfill ambition. It gives strength to face competition and encourages working tirelessly for success. It is a pushing energy that uses force to overcome adverse circumstances, therefore, Mars is not afraid of fear and never surrender in front of circumstances. The Sun, the Moon, and Jupiter are friends of Mars, while the relationship with Venus and Saturn is neutral. Mars' enemies are Mercury and Rahu, which means that force can be defeated by intelligence and deceit. History offers many examples where, upon failing to defeat the opposing side through the use of force, the other party attempts to secure victory by resorting to deceit, trickery, and diplomacy.

6.1 Mars in the Birth Chart

Mars is the planet of energy and a symbol of desire. The position of Mars in the birth chart determines how an individual fulfills their desires and how they face conflicts or challenges.

- **Fire Signs (Aries, Leo, Sagittarius):** These individuals possess a straightforward and spirited nature. They tend to act impulsively and often make decisions very quickly. They face challenges head-on and never give up, although they may struggle to maintain patience.

- **Earth signs (Taurus, Virgo, Capricorn):** They have a practical and steadfast outlook. They prefer to keep things organized and in their proper places. They strive for tangible results and security.

- **Air signs (Gemini, Libra, Aquarius):** They primarily use their intellect and communication skills to get their way. They are adept at debating, negotiating, and bargaining to fulfill their desires.
- **Water signs (Cancer, Scorpio, Pisces):** For individuals belonging to these signs, emotions, feelings, and intuition are of great importance. They are compassionate and loving, yet their moods fluctuate rapidly, and they can easily become irritable. They protect their loved ones with unwavering loyalty and act based on their emotions rather than logic.

6.2 Exaltation and Debilitation

Mars becomes exalted at 28 degrees in Capricorn and debilitated at 28 degrees in Cancer. Among the three earthy signs, Capricorn is the last earthy sign that has the most grip. Ruled by Saturn, it is the strongest earthy sign that has a strong capacity to make full use of available resources. This sign indicates working hard and the maximum utilization of every possible resource.

Where there is energy, it must be controlled, and to achieve maximum results, energy should be utilized properly. In Capricorn, Martian energy is fully utilized at 28 degrees; therefore, it is the exaltation point of Mars. Mars starts losing its power in Cancer and loses its entire energy at 28 degrees; therefore, it is the debilitation sign of Mars.

6.3 Positive, Negative and Detrimental Sign

Mars rules Aries and Scorpio, where the former is its positive sign and the latter its negative sign. The positive sign indicates aggression, but it also shows that the person forgives when asked. Whereas in the negative sign, the feeling of revenge remains suppressed, and when the time comes, it attacks the enemy stealthily and lethally.

Taurus and Libra are considered to be detrimental signs of Mars. In astrology, when a planet is positioned in the sign directly opposite the one it rules (i.e., its own house), it is considered to be in a state of 'detriment'. Mars rules both Aries and Scorpio. Since Taurus lies directly opposite Scorpio and Libra lies directly opposite Aries, Mars is compelled to operate contrary to its natural disposition in these two signs.

Taurus is a slow-paced, methodical, and stable earth sign. Mars is a fast-acting planet that seeks to bring about change through immediate action, whereas Taurus prioritizes peace and stability. Consequently, Martian energy feels frustrated when Taurus fails to take action; it keeps fuming inwardly, yet circumstances do not work in its favor.

Libra is associated with balance, deals, and partnerships, whereas Mars's energy is direct and independent. This placement of Mars compels the individual to engage in negotiations and deal-making; consequently, they often find themselves in stressful situations where they are forced to agree to terms they would rather not accept.

6.4 Strong Mars in Different Houses

Mars is very strong in the 10th House, where it attains Digbala (directional strength). The aspect of Mars in the 10th house makes a person very active in worldly affairs and motivates them to take the initiative. It is also highly powerful in the 1st, 3rd, 6th, and 11th houses.

1st House (Self & Vitality): The first house relates to physical constitution and appearance. This placement of Mars makes a person highly courageous, self-confident, and impressive. In this house, Mars bestows a strong and energetic physique. Such an individual is very ambitious and works hard to fulfill their desires. They possess excellent administrative qualities. However, if Mars is afflicted, the person may become arrogant and stubborn.

3rd House (Courage & Siblings): The third house governs the practical application of the mind, thought processes, curiosity, communication, and the immediate environment (including neighbors). This makes a person very active, fearless, and outspoken. In such a situation, the person has to undertake several short journeys.

It is an important house through which an individual transforms their thoughts and ideas into creative endeavors. Ideally, this house should remain unoccupied, as the presence of malefic planets here can lead a person to misuse their mind. Consequently, a weak Mars in this house is considered unfavorable. If the individual's Moon is also weak, their mental strength may be diminished. Such a situation often leads to conflicts and disputes, and an inability to focus prevents the person from engaging in any creative work.

6th House (Enemies & Health): This placement is excellent for winning competitions, overcoming obstacles, and facing challenges. Mars instills the fighting spirit needed to surmount hurdles. Such a person does not shy away from confrontation and stands up against injustice. A strong influence of Mars can lead a person to become a military man, lawyer, athlete, or surgeon.

10th House (Career & Authority): This is the best position for Mars. It provides abundant energy and generates tremendous potential for leadership, ambition, and success in fields such as defense, sports, or executive roles. However, focusing too heavily on professional goals and public life sometimes leads to the neglect of other important aspects of life.

11th House (Desires & Gains): The 11th house is the house of gains; consequently, under this influence, the native works very hard to earn money and ensures a steady flow of income. This position of Mars provides abundant energy to fulfill desires. However, a habit of reckless spending and a lavish lifestyle can deplete these resources quickly.

6.5 Jupiter and Mars

Energy can give both positive and negative results, and it depends on its use. Uncontrolled and directionless energy can create problems. Jupiter is the planet that gives direction. Energy always requires the right direction. When energy gets direction, it gives positive results. Therefore, if both Mars and Jupiter are favorably positioned in the horoscope, the results can be excellent. Such an individual can achieve great success in life, possessing all the qualities needed to assess associated risks and make prudent decisions.

Therefore, along with the position of Mars, it is important to see the position and strength of Jupiter as well. The house in which they both aspect, the person receives the right direction in matters related to that house, and he always makes energetic and wise decisions.

6.6 Venus and Mars

Mars represents the raw physical energy present in our bodies. It is the ruler of sexual desire, while Venus is the ruler of attraction. Sexual energy is what drives the world. It is through this energy that one becomes two, two becomes three, and four and the world expands. Sexual energy gives rise to the expansion of the world. If used and channeled properly, this energy can yield excellent results. Whatever exists in its original form always needs to be refined, cleansed, and polished. Venus represents love, and love has the immense potential to transform a person.

Therefore, the feminine energy of Venus has the immense potential to transform the masculine, raw energy of Mars. When Venus is in conjunction with Mars or when Venus aspects Mars, the work of transforming this raw energy begins. Feminine energy is passive; therefore, Venus does not take any action; its mere presence is enough to transform the raw energy of Mars.

Therefore, in the presence of a woman, men immediately stop quarreling and start pretending to be gentlemen.

However, a downside to this is that If Mars is in Taurus or Libra (signs ruled by Venus) and is aspected by malefic planets and Venus, the individual's libido may become excessive or distorted, potentially leading to sexually perverted behavior. This can result in an intense surge in sexual desire, a disregard for emotional boundaries, or the emergence of bizarre sexual urges. Such individuals may become cruel, ruthless, merciless, and may engage in criminal activities.

6.7 Mars Produces Prostitutes

"The 4th house rules chastity and the 7th house governs marital happiness. If Mars and Venus conjoin in the 4th house or the 7th house and are affected by Saturn, then the native may turn into a sexual pervert or a prostitute, provided that the 4th or the 7th house must be either in Mars's sign or Venus's sign. If the 4th or the 7th house is too much afflicted by malefics, then the native may marry twice or thrice, still, he may not get any peace at home." (Dr. Nimai Banerjee - Planetary Behaviour & Human Life, Written by N.N. Saha, Page – 13)

6.8 Mars Makes Top Business Executives

"The lord of the 1st, 5th and the 10th house must be placed in angular or trine houses to become a top business executive. If any of these three lords is placed in a trik house (6th, 8th or 12th), the native may not get the desired result."

"Mars is a strong dynamic planet. It gives executive ability, high ambition, dynamic energy, great stamina, strength and power, ability to undertake any risky adventure, and strong will power, if posited in a strong angular house i.e., 1st or 10th house. Conjunction of Mars and Rahu, the sun and Mars, Mars and Jupiter, Mars and Mercury, or Mars and the Moon in the first or the 10th house makes top business executives, high Govt. officials or great political leaders." (Dr. Nimai Banerjee - Planetary Behaviour & Human Life, Written by N.N. Saha, Page – 9 & 13)

6.9 Mars & Wealth

Mars is the warrior planet and has no direct connection to wealth. It is related with heat and movement of energy. It is the planet of action and governs;

- Ambition, drive and energy to earn
- Willingness to take financial risks
- Business involving land, real estate, and property

Mars shapes one's earning potential through initiative and action. It determines how an individual channel their energy to achieve what they desire. It equips you with the ability to handle pressure and succeed in competitive environments.

6.10 Mars - The Planet of Outward Activity

Mars is the planet of external activities and our primal, inner desires; it governs outward actions and is driven by the urge to conquer. As a planet with a fiery and masculine nature, it is directly linked to aggression, this makes its regulation important. On the positive side, this energy highlights the importance of fulfilling external tasks and responsibilities, emphasizing persistent effort and determination across various aspects of life.

In Hindi, it is called 'Mangal', which means 'auspicious'. It implies that, by nature, this innocent energy is auspicious–unless a person turns it into inauspicious. Therefore, when Mars yields auspicious results, it redirects the individual's immense power away from aggression and toward constructive and protective actions. An innocence comes alive within an immensely powerful individual. This controlled energy helps the person shed destructive tendencies, thereby revealing the pure, childlike honesty, clarity, and grace within them.

However, Mars signifies more than just anger, conflict, or confrontation; it represents the fire that ignites our creative life force. This energy drives us to move forward in life and compels us to persevere until we achieve our goals. It governs our physical energy, stamina, sexual desire, and our ability to prove ourselves across various spheres of life. It determines how we handle competition, pressure, and conflict, as well as the direction in which we channel that aggression. Mars shapes our passions, which can manifest as either creative or destructive forces. The tenth house of the birth chart is the most significant house for external activities; consequently, the influence of Mars on this house produces an individual who remains highly active in the external world.

6.11 Saturn and Mars

The energy of Mars always needs control, and Saturn is the planet of control and restrictions. The conjunction or aspect of Saturn on natal Mars controls its energy. The cold planet Saturn calms and controls the anger of Mars. The conjunction of Saturn and Mars indicates that the person will suppress his anger and will act only when the time comes, but suppressing anger for a long time also indicates an explosion one day.

For example, we can understand this conjunction as a hot iron rod dipped in the ice-cold water. Fire and water are enemies to each other, and the meeting of extremely hot and extremely cold things causes a sudden explosion. Therefore, people having this conjunction are sometimes unable to control their anger and their suppressed thoughts erupt someday, and they suddenly commit a crime. It is necessary to analyze the strength of the Moon because a strong mind is necessary to control violent thoughts. Criminals who have this conjunction often regret committing crimes. They moved impulsively and repented later. If surrounded by malefic planets, this combination produces many negative results, and such a person gets angry very quickly.

Saturn creates delay, and Mars is impulsive to act. These are two opposite energies. Mars is the push energy, and Saturn is the pull energy. When these two energies work simultaneously, then the door will not open. Sometimes, these people act impulsively to get quick results, and later their outcome gets delayed. It also indicates a career break, and it takes time to open the new door because Saturn is the significator (karaka) of the 10th house. On the positive side, this energy indicates dedication, hard work, and long-term success with consistent efforts and proper planning.

6.12 Mars is a Bachelor Planet

Mars is considered a bachelor planet and represents celibacy. Therefore, its placement in the 7th house or its conjunction with the lord of the 7th house indicates a delay in marriage or a life of celibacy after marriage. Saturn signifies penance, and Mars signifies austerity and inner fire. This conjunction can produce good results on the path of spirituality if this energy is utilized properly. The energy of Mars compels the individual to take initiative. It is the assertive and adventurous energy. Mars is the drive that forces one to leave the comfort of the bed in the early morning and become active.

6.13 Mars - The planet of Success

The position of Mars in the horoscope indicates the willingness to work, as Mars represents the desire of the individual. Therefore, the position of Mars according to the sign and house indicates the energy to achieve the desire. Energy is required to make efforts, and when the energy is high, one can take risks, and this is necessary for self-expression. Mars represents the blood flowing in our veins, which gives us the energy to fight and survive in this world. The passion of Mars is necessary to fight and succeed in a competition. The flow of blood manifests life and makes all kinds of progress and growth possible. Therefore, a strong Mars in the horoscope is essential to be proactive and determined, which are essential qualities of a successful person. A weak Mars indicates dissipation of energy, lack of courage, and a tendency towards backwardness.

6.14 Mars - Catalyst for Professional Success

An unafflicted Mars imparts many good qualities: self-confidence, stamina, ability to understand risk and take initiative, accept challenges and perform heroic deeds, independent spirit, fighting, courage, boldness, etc. A strong Mars indicates that the native has good physical strength and can be a good sportsperson. A strong and positive Mars is essential in astrology as the primary engine for professional success.

The power of Mars profoundly influences how an individual confronts challenges and fulfills his ambitions:

- **Initiative and Leadership:** A well-placed Mars bestows the courage to take charge, make decisive decisions, and lead a team effectively.
- **Resilience:** Mars provides the mental and physical stamina required to navigate through obstacles or difficult phases encountered in one's professional life.
- **Competitive Edge:** Mars fuels the desire to win and to excel as the best in one's chosen field, enabling the individual to stand out amidst the competition.

In the horoscope, the position of Mars indicates the energy present in that house, and its aspect indicates that the individual will take initiative to overcome obstacles. The position and strength of Mars and its aspect show the areas of life where the person likes to take the initiative and utilize the energy. The readiness to compete and the ability to face difficult situations are determined by the sign and house ruled by Mars.

Therefore, this energy must always be channeled constructively. Mars attains its exaltation in the sign of Capricorn at 28 degrees – a placement that precisely embodies the proper utilization of this energy. This clearly indicates that the energy of Mars can yield excellent results, but it is essential to control it; that is why Mars is considered a significator of professional success.

6.15 Mars - The Fiery Energy

Mars is a powerful symbol of dynamic energy, courage, and unwavering determination. This fiery planet acts like an engine, providing the physical stamina and courage essential for professional success. It fosters new initiatives and inspires proactive action. It supports bold decisions made with clarity rather than hesitation. It helps one stand firm in the face of difficulties and fight for one's goals with steadfast determination.

The energy of Mars is deeply linked to professions that demand strength, discipline, and control, even under pressure. It is associated with roles requiring focus, precision, and determination. It relates to fields such as surgery, emergency, and dentistry, which call for quick thinking alongside a steady mind and hands. Consequently, individuals with an afflicted Mars tend to panic easily and struggle to handle emergency situations.

This dynamic energy fosters a warrior-like mindset, often leading individuals to pursue careers in the military or police forces. It is an action-oriented energy linked to entrepreneurship and technical environments. It cultivates a mind adept at taking initiative, this helps in making quick decisions and taking risks, which is essential for executive and leadership roles.

This energy helps in solving technical problems, paving the way for careers in engineering and construction. Its association with machinery and speed makes it highly beneficial for mechanical and automotive engineering. It is linked to sports that require physical stamina and a competitive spirit. This fiery energy proves valuable in any field demanding enthusiasm and zeal. Careers in law enforcement agencies and security services are also associated with Mars.

With the help of controlled energy, an individual can work under pressure without succumbing to panic. This protective energy aids people, save lives, and yields tangible results capable of transforming lives. It operates in settings ranging from the operating room–amidst surgical instruments–to the battlefield, amidst bullets and weaponry; in both instances, precision coupled with a steady mind is essential, for only a stable hand can strike the target accurately.

Mars provides the inner strength needed to move forward fearlessly. However, uncontrolled energy gets wasted in futile disputes. Therefore, it is essential for Mars to be well-placed in the horoscope, as an adverse placement can lead to negative outcomes.

The journey to success in life requires immense strength, which an afflicted Mars cannot provide. Thus, it is essential to channel this energy in the right direction and make every effort to prevent its wastage; the exaltation of Mars in the sign of Capricorn at 28 degrees exemplifies this state.

6.16 Mars - The Own Boss

Mars symbolizes action, ambition, drive and power. A strong Martian influence makes an individual highly action-oriented, prioritizing direct execution and rapid completion of tasks. Mars governs the spirit of entrepreneurship and provides the courage to start a new venture, move forward despite financial uncertainty, and sustain it. If Mars is positioned in the first, eighth, or tenth house in its own sign, a friendly sign, or its sign of exaltation, it instills a drive to excel in the business world, and the individual earns respect through their hard work and dedication. This fiery planet strengthens our muscles and instills in us the drive to emerge victorious by facing intense competition.

Mars dislikes excessive paperwork or bureaucracy; consequently, such a person does not appreciate a boss who emphasizes documentation over actual work or insists on strict adherence to protocol. Thus, a strong

Martian influence (particularly in Aries, Scorpio, or Capricorn) fosters boldness and a focus on results, rather than a tendency to merely talk, seek absolute certainty in everything, or back down.

Consequently, such individuals dislike being bossed around. Their mindset resembles that of a commander-in-chief whose sole objective is to win a war; they devise the strategy for victory, while others are expected to execute the orders. Mars asserts, "I alone shall give the orders."

These people perform best when running their own business or holding a position where they can guide the work of others. They know exactly how to get the task done but strongly dislike interference from others while doing so. Since they cannot tolerate being constrained for long periods, they become frustrated in environments characterized by micromanagement and prefer to leave such situations.

The high energy of Mars dispels the fear of failure and, instead of following others' orders, empowers one to become their own boss with self-confidence. Martian energy force us to rise and move forward in life, rather than simply waiting. This energy helps in starting something from scratch and growing and making it big. Being highly inventive and mechanically inclined, they excel as designers, manufacturers, managers, administrators and business leaders, dedicating themselves wholeheartedly to any task they undertake. Thus, they achieve greater success in roles that offer them the freedom to make decisions independently.

6.17 Mars and Conflicts

When this warrior planet is afflicted, it easily gives rise to quarrels, power struggles, and open confrontations. Anger is primarily associated with Mars, and its affliction leaves the individual unable to control his temper. The specific house and zodiac sign occupied by Mars in the birth chart reveal exactly where and over what issues you are most likely to get embroiled in bitter disputes. The 8th house is the house of transformation; therefore, the 8th aspect of Mars is considered a major trigger for sudden conflict.

This fiery planet can either strengthen relationships or ignite conflicts. For instance, Mars in the second house might inspire a person to embrace family values and build strong relationships, or it could trigger family disputes over money and family resources. A weak and afflicted Mars can lead to the following outcomes:

- A tendency to get angry easily
- Reacting impulsively and in a hurtful manner
- Marital discord
- Frequent arguments in relationships
- Tense, competitive, or hostile relationships with siblings
- Power struggles with a partner or family members
- Susceptibility to high blood pressure, cuts, and burns
- Accidents or injuries involving bleeding

Misusing the energy of Mars diminishes its potential to yield positive results. It reduces a person's endurance and makes their temperament irritable. When this energy exerts a negative influence, it can lead to recurring injuries, burns, or accidents. It creates a likelihood of constant friction with teammates or partners. The individual's ability to listen to others diminishes; such people tend to talk excessively and remain adamant about having their own way. They are often restless and always ready to pick a fight with anyone.

When this volatile energy becomes unbalanced and uncontrolled, it leads to heated arguments, emotional clashes, and attempts by partners to dominate others. When an argument begins, they speak rapidly, yet neither party listens to the other. When the energy of Mars is excessively active or unbalanced, it is often linked to elevated cortisol levels (the stress hormone) or a hyperactive nervous system—manifesting as physical restlessness, anger, and pent-up energy that makes it difficult to find peace or relaxation at home.

6.18 Mars Produces Violent Criminals

"When Mars becomes weak by its position in houses - 3rd / 6th / 8th / 12th in a nativity, it makes one cruel, brutal, hard-hearted, unkind, unjust, hostile, aggressive etc. Single Mars can't become so much evil. But its conjunction with some other two malefics i.e., Saturn and Rahu or Saturn and Ketu in an evil house, is very dangerous. It then produces violent criminals, as Mars is a planet of violent aggression, hostility, brutality, vindictiveness etc.; if posited in Venus's sign." (Dr. Nimai Banerjee - Planetary Behaviour & Human Life, Written by N.N. Saha, Page – 14)

6.19 Basic Instincts

Mars governs our fundamental nature—such as anger, aggression, sex, conflict, and the survival instinct. It is associated to the basic body attraction. This raw energy immediately surfaces when faced with adversity or challenges. When it comes to survival, this energy compels immediate action. It uses force to quickly eliminate challenges. With Mars, no thought or deliberation goes into undertaking any task.

Consequently, deep contemplation is not the domain of Mars. On the one hand, it is good; it is a protective energy that uses its power to protect a person by taking immediate action in times of danger. On the other hand, its impulsiveness, uncontrolled anger, and aggression can also wreak havoc. Impulsiveness and anger consume a person; therefore, Mars is both a protector and a predator.

6.20 Why is Mars considered a malefic planet?

The main difference between malefic and benefic planets is – "Give and Take". Jupiter, Moon, Mercury, and Venus are considered auspicious planets because they give. These planets provide beneficial qualities and help in survival and growth. Their first quality is giving; hence, their transits and aspects are considered auspicious and produce favorable results. They also give inauspicious results, but that is not their first quality. Jupiter provides good luck, auspiciousness, marriage, and children. Moon provides emotional stability, imagination, a beautiful appearance, sensitivity, and nurturing ability. Venus gives love, luxury, comfort, and charm. Mercury provides intelligence, logic, communication, mental agility, etc.

The first purpose of malefic planets is not to give to a person but to take from him. People run away from the taker and wait for the giver to come. Saturn, Mars, Rahu and Ketu are considered malefic planets because their transit or aspect first takes or removes, or separates something from life. These planets are also capable of giving and doing good in a person's life, but this is not their primary purpose. Saturn gives pressure and pain before doing something good. Rahu and Ketu create unrest and separation. Rahu first brings confusion, and Ketu detachment. About Mars, some important characteristics are given below;

- Mars, the god of war, does not think twice before action.
- Mars loves challenges and does not contemplate before action.
- Mars language of thinking is use of force.
- The task has to be accomplished at any cost, and the obstacle has to be pushed aside.
- Mars way of working is use of force.
- Mars way is to achieve the goal by using force.

Mars is considered a malefic planet because of the following reasons;

1. The energy of Mars is uncontrolled, directionless, and impulsive.
2. Mars is associated with anger, which is not a constructive energy.
3. Mars is the lord of weapons and war. Weapons in the hands of an angry and directionless person are dangerous.
4. Mars causes loss of blood and accidents.
5. Mars always removes obstacles by using force and does not care about the damage caused.
6. The main objective of Mars is to win by using force, no matter how much destruction it has to cause.
7. This fiery and aggressive energy cause conflict and impulsive decisions and do not bother about outcome.
8. When its influence is adverse, it can result in physical injuries, and disputes.

6.21 Mars - The Negative Side

On the negative side, it is impatient, impulsive, and quarrelsome. An afflicted and weak Mars indicates that the native lacks the necessary positive skills and fails to rise high. The person will use his strength to fulfill his desires and can go to any extent. Irrespective of how many fingers are burnt, the fulfilment of desire is important for him, and if the person is running on the Mahadasha of Mars, then dangerous consequences can be possible, as he is not ready to give up his desire under any circumstances.

An afflicted Mars indicates that the native tends to lose his temper easily and, without a second thought, begins to verbally abuse others. Such an individual possesses a quarrelsome nature and remains ready to pick a fight over even the most trivial matters. Such people lack listening skills and are more interested in talking incessantly. For instance, people are prepared to engage in a street fight over something as minor as a small scratch on their car.

The afflicted Mars does not like differences of opinion with anyone. The native argues in vain; instead of giving any intelligent argument, he prefers to use abuses and force and feels the joy of winning the argument (battle). These natives are perpetually ready to fight, regardless of the issue at hand. This impulsive and combative temperament signifies that Mars occupies a weak position in the horoscope.

While a strong Mars signifies an individual endowed with immense courage, endurance, and zeal. Rather than becoming entangled in petty troubles and disputes, a strong Mars grants a person the mental fortitude and self-control needed to rise above trivial matters and focus their energy on achieving major goals.

An afflicted Mars indicates that a person may be prone to a quick temper. Those unable to control their anger and impulses often inadvertently harm their goals, damage their relationships, and derail their life trajectory and outcome. Constant entanglement in various disputes and conflicts creates a distance from success in life, as a strong Mars is essential for achieving success. A strong Mars transforms desires into action, whereas a weak Mars can lead to procrastination, a fear of moving forward, and an unwillingness to take risks.

6.22 The Aspect of Mars

The energy of Mars acts as a push. When there is an ambition to be achieved or a problem to be solved, Mars takes the initiative. This energy uses force to overcome problems and bring about solutions.

6.22.1 The 4th Aspect

The fourth house is the house of peace, and the fourth aspect of Mars provides peace and harmony by force. It is the most energetic aspect that calms disruptions by force and brings peace. Mars represents desire, with its fourth aspect, a person puts all his energy into removing obstacles in fulfilling his desire.

For example, let's say Mars is placed in the ascendant in Aries and its fourth aspect is on the fourth house, which is the house of peace, and among the body parts, it is related to the heart. The first sign, Aries, is a fire sign, and the fourth sign, Cancer, is a water sign. The relationship between fire and water is hostile. If the problem arises related to the fourth house (home), then Mars will solve it only by using force. To bring peace at home, such a person may even beat his family member.

Mars in the 1st house means the person will take initiative in odd circumstances to maintain peace, and for that, he will use force. The 4th house is related to the heart, and if there is a blockage in the flow of blood, Mars will initiate surgery to clear the blockage and give relief to the person. Mars is the lord of weapons, and do not hesitate to use weapons if necessary to maintain peace. A cardiac operation is the use of medical instruments on the chest to remove obstacles that are hindrances to the flow of blood and bring peace to the person.

6.22.2 The 7th Aspect

The 7th aspect of any planet indicates support for that house. Mars's support is direct and related to courage and bravery. Mars is related to the younger brother. If Mars is good in a person's horoscope, then the person will get support from their younger brother at a time of difficulty. For example, if Mars is placed in the 1st house, the person will provide his full support to his spouse and encourage her to take initiative and move forward.

The 7th element in the zodiac is a complementary element like; Fire (1) - Air (7), Earth (2) - Water (8), Air (3) - Fire (9), Water (4) - Earth (10) and represents the same quality, like; Movable - Movable, Fixed - Fixed, Dual - Dual.

Aries is the first sign, which is a Fire and Movable sign. From here, 180° apart, is the 7th sign, Libra, which is an

Air and Movable sign. The elements in these two signs are complementary to each other, Fire and Air, and both have the same quality-movable.

The energy generated by a planet in Aries is different from the same planet produced in Libra, as the element is different. Hence, such an aspect creates pressure, tension, and conflict in life as there is a lack of harmony between these two energies. For example, Mars, which is a hot planet in the fire sign (Aries), produces a different kind of energy in the natal chart, and Saturn in the Air sign (Libra) produces a different kind of energy in transit in the 7th house and there is no harmony between these two energies. Although the element supports each other, planetary energy is different. When Saturn in transit creates a 7th aspect with the natal Mars, various tensions and conflicts start to arise in the life of the natives related to the matter of the concerned house.

In the same manner, Mars in Taurus, which is Earth and a Fixed sign, creates opposition to Scorpio, which is Water and a Fixed sign, and so on. Due to disharmony of energies, although the opposition (7th) aspect creates stress, pressure, the difference of opinion, and conflict in life, but element supports each other, so support also comes. Also, both the signs have the same quality; therefore, deep inside they feel attraction toward each other: Movable (1) - Movable (7), Fixed (2) – Fixed (8), Dual (3) – Dual (9).

This is why it is said that opposites attract. Each house from the seventh house represents not only tension and conflict but also attraction and support. The first house in the zodiac represents yourself, and the seventh house represents your spouse or partner. Lovers attract and support each other, but stress, tension, and differences of opinion are also a part of life from which one cannot escape. It is the functioning of the opposite aspect (7th) that will accompany you, due to which you will feel the attraction, but will also give stress and tension in life.

The 7th Aspect:

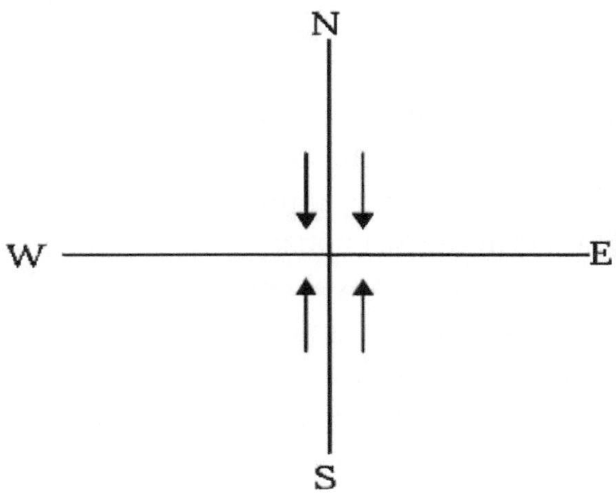

The above chart represents the energy coming from two different directions. Such a situation in life teaches us to create balance in every sphere of life. The opposition represents the polarities, and without balance, it cannot exist. It is the meeting of two opposite energies, like yin and yang. When two opposite energies of similar quality meet, it provides an opportunity for a union. It also indicates a compromise without which a union of two different energies is not possible, and then such a situation becomes a stalemate in life.

6.22.3 The 8th Aspect

The 8th house is the house of death, and death is a transformation. A new life begins after death, and the past has gone forever. The 8th house is all about hidden matters of life. It is a secretive house related to investigation, research, psychology, hidden knowledge, occult sciences, etc. Therefore, Mars' 8th aspect means transformation, and this energy pushes the person to transformation in the matters where Mars' 8th aspect falls.

Mars in the ascendant indicates that some such events will occur in the life of the person, which will change their life forever, and a new approach towards life will be born. If Mars is in the 8th house, then transformation is related to the 3rd house, which is the house of communication, siblings, and transportation. The 8th aspect of Mars brings accident, sudden loss, or any other change in life, and that event transforms the person forever.

To uncover the hidden things, one needs to enter the dark, and for that, courage is required at every step. Mars – the planet of courage, forces the person to go ahead even when circumstances are not in favor. When a person takes steps to go and find out the hidden things, their transformation begins in life. When the person is aware of the hidden matters, occult knowledge, or research and findings, their life is completely transformed. After knowing the hidden truth, he will not be the same person. As death transforms the person, knowledge about the hidden truth also transforms the person completely.

Secrets are always kept confidential because they have the potential to change a person. That is why nature keeps secrets hidden, and only those who have courage can enter this path. When the secrets are in a person's hands, he cannot remain the same person who started the journey to enter the darkness. Now he has something in his hands that others do not have, and this knowledge has the potential to change a person's life forever.

Therefore, the eighth aspect of Mars is transformative. Whatever house its eighth aspect falls on, transformation is inevitable. But the process of transformation is not easy, it brings disruption and pain. When it is activated, various changes begin in a person's life, and he is unable to understand the functioning of Mars. After this process, the person comes to know the hidden truth. He is aware of the knowledge that is necessary for his life. According to the author, this may be the reason why ancient sages have given the 4th and the 8th aspects to Mars.

The Aspect of Mars

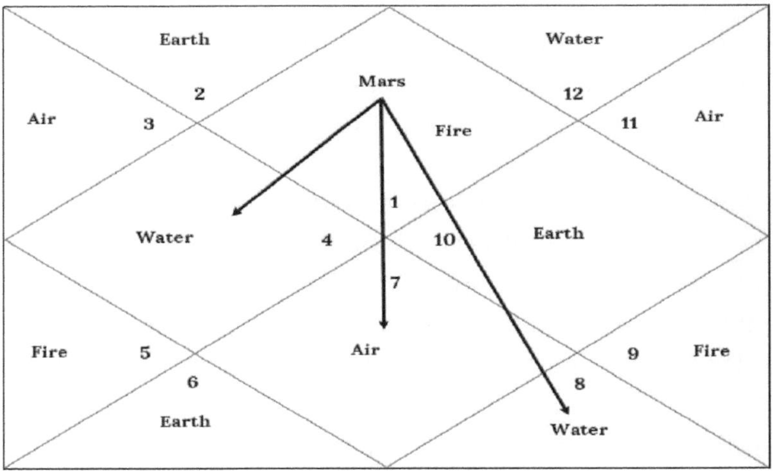

Chapter 7

Jupiter & Rahu: The Same Aspects

Jupiter is considered the most auspicious planet in astrology. It is a watery planet. It is a highly benefic planet and represents optimism, buoyancy, and expansion. The planet of abundance is noble and benevolent. It bestows honor, fame, and prestige. It represents honesty, faith, morality, spirituality, and devotion. It represents the future.

Rahu is the lord of illusions. It is the master of dishonesty and never shows its true face to others. It represents overnight fame and popularity, glamour, media sensation, material success, hallucination, psychosis, paranoia, etc. It is always hungry and is never satisfied, no matter how much it accumulates. Rahu always thinks about the future, and its position in the horoscope indicates that the person wants to experience things that they do not have yet. Like Jupiter, Rahu also represents the future. In Vedic astrology, Jupiter has been assigned three aspects: 5th, 7th, and 9th, and Rahu has also been assigned the same aspects.

Here the question arises that;

1. Both these planets represent the future, so what is the difference between them?

2. What is the difference between the 5th, 7th and 9th aspect of Jupiter and Rahu?

3. Why have the ancient sages assigned a same aspect to these two planets–where one is the lord of honesty, while the other is the lord of dishonesty?

We can understand this with the help of a coin. Only one side of the coin can be seen at a time, and the other side is right behind it but cannot be seen. Jupiter represents truth, and Rahu is the lord of untruth. When a person sees untruth, he does not know the truth, and when the truth is known, the untruth disappears. These two are completely opposites, and the existence of one eliminates the other.

Rahu is the lord of illusion, and Jupiter is the lord of wisdom. As long as illusion is visible, wisdom is absent, and when wisdom comes, illusion disappears. Both Jupiter and Rahu show the future, but one shows truth and the other untruth. Jupiter symbolizes honesty, and Rahu dishonesty. The choice between these two options is in the hands of the individual. He can choose between honesty and dishonesty, and both options always exist together. A person's choice determines the direction of his future. Therefore, the ancient scriptures rightly say that Jupiter and Rahu both show the future, but one is the lord of truth, the other of falsehood.

Rahu is the expansion of Maya and Jupiter is the expansion of religion and knowledge. Wherever truth exists, untruth also exists. The difference is only in vision, and as soon as vision becomes clear, untruth immediately disappears. The moment truth is revealed, everything changes. Therefore, Rahu exists only as long as it remains hidden; as soon as truth is realized, it immediately disappears.

Therefore, Rahu's power lies in operating covertly, and deep, dense darkness is the very source of that power. Its strength stems from never revealing its true identity. Rahu makes every possible effort to fulfill its suppressed desires; it constantly seeks an opportunity and vanishes the moment its objective is achieved. For this reason, it is designated as a 'shadow planet' in astrology. Its nature is to shun the truth and always align with falsehood.

Jupiter, on the other hand, detests lies of any kind. The solar system's largest planet is a symbol of truth–a truth that runs very deep. Ultimate truth encompasses the entirety of reality–vast, complex, and difficult to comprehend. Grasping the concept of reality is a monumental journey, and every small fragment of truth gained represents a step forward on that infinite path.

Consequently, there is a 180-degree difference between truth and falsehood—much like how flipping a coin 180 degrees reveals its other side. The truth is revealed only by moving 180 degrees away from falsehood. Thus, according to the author, there is a 180-degree separation between Rahu and Ketu: one is the lord of *Maya* (illusion), while the other is the lord of *Moksha* (liberation).

Ancient texts state that as long as Maya reigns within a person, they wander in the world. As soon as Maya is removed, the world ends, and the infinite expanse of knowledge is born. Truth and untruth are two sides of the same coin, the difference being only in perspective. Therefore, according to the author ancient sages assign the same aspect to both planets.

<u>The Aspect of Jupiter & Rahu</u>

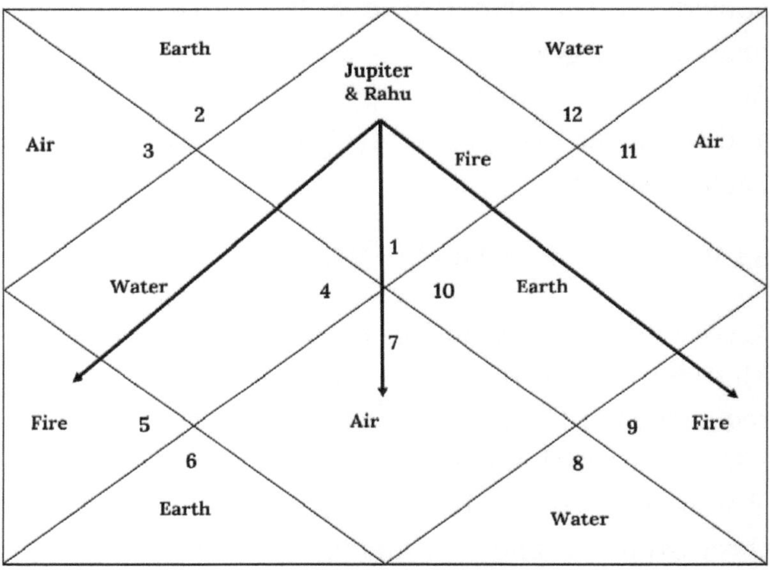

Chapter 8

Venus: The One-Eyed Planet

Venus is considered the guru of demons. It is considered the planet of love. It bestows marriage, beauty, and grace. It bestows luxury and comfort. According to Hindu mythology, Venus has only one eye, and its other eye was destroyed by Lord Vishnu in Vamana avatar.

8.1 Puranic Story related to Venus

According to the mythological story, there was a demon King Bali, who ruled both the earth and heaven. The gods requested Lord Vishnu to free them from King Bali. Lord Vishnu then took the form of a dwarf Brahmin (Vamana avatar), went to King Bali, and requested him to donate three steps of land. The demon guru, Shukracharya, immediately understood Lord Vishnu's trick and advised King Bali against granting him his request. However, Bali accepted Vamana's request and, to fulfill it, asked for permission to wash his feet with water. Shukracharya then entered the vessel and stopped the flow of water, preventing Vamana's request from being fulfilled. To clear the blocked flow, Lord Vishnu took a blade of grass and poked out one of Guru Shukracharya's eyes.

Significance of the Story

This mythological story holds a lot of importance regarding the functioning of the planet Venus. This story tells us that love has only one eye. Two eyes can discern differences, and love knows no difference; love cannot think logically. Our eyes are connected to the brain, and the brain can think and understand, which love does not have. Love knows no distinctions; love is the joy of oneness where all distinctions disappear.

The sight of one eye means there is no more discrimination. There is no more thinking and understanding; only love is present. According to author, when Guru Shukracharya understood this difference, Lord Vishnu took away one of his eyes, because discerning is not Venus's job.

8.2 Venus in Shravana Nakshatra

The deity of Shravan Nakshatra is Lord Vishnu, who is associated with the Vamana avatar. In the Vamana avatar, Lord Vishnu destroyed one of Shukracharya's eyes.

Therefore, if Venus is placed in Shravan Nakshatra in a person's horoscope, the person may be born with only one eye, or may have a defect in one eye, or may lose vision in one eye due to an accident.

8.3 Venus – The Planet of Love

The lack of vision in one of Venus' eyes is a symbolic representation of the fact that Venus has no logic, as love is a feeling that cannot be expressed in words. Vision in only one eye signifies the experience of love without question, because when oneness is realized, all questions cease. This is why people with Venusian traits are weak in logical subjects such as mathematics.

Venus is the planet of love and love can only be felt, not understood by logic. Love is;

- Love cannot have two thoughts.
- Love cannot look in two different directions.
- Love does not know the difference between small or big.
- Love does not know the difference between logical or irrational, love means only love.
- Love has nothing to do with the brain, which creates logic.
- Love has nothing to do with the mind, which can think in many directions; these are two different paths.

The mind craves logic, and love craves totality, and this is possible only when you look at the "One" without any distinction, because 'One' means that all distinctions have now ceased to exist. Venus's single eye represents complete dedication and concentration without any distraction. Our both eyes create the ability to see distinctions, which is why people close one eye while aiming. You can do one small experiment - Close one eye and try to line up your two index fingers from different directions. You'll be surprised to find that the exact match isn't there. There's always a slight difference because one eye can't detect that slight difference. Therefore,

- Love does not know the difference between the two.
- Love is a feeling for which a person is ready to make any sacrifice.
- Love is a feeling of totality in which lovers forget all differences.
- Love is a feeling of oneness and on the higher aspect it becomes divine.

At its deepest level, love is called 'divine,' because it transcends the ego, demand, and personal gain. Love recognizes only feelings and remains indifferent to the source from which those feelings arise. Love does not understand structured and systematic patterns because it defies logics and rigid timelines. Consequently, an individual under the influence of Venus often operates within flexible and rhythmic frameworks, rather than strictly adhering to fixed deadlines.

Therefore, a person with a calculative mindset stays away from Venus-related activities and cannot understand love. Venus means where distinctions end, and where distinctions end, duality ends. Therefore, Venus is exalted in Pisces at 27 degrees, where all duality ends and the seeker of the truth attains a state of eternal bliss. Therefore, the ancient scriptures say that "He" (God) is not two, this world is an expansion of the "One".

In the above story, Guru Shukracharya used logic to conclude that there was something wrong with Vamana Brahmin's request for three steps of land. He recognized the distinction through logic. Drawing conclusions based on facts is the mind's job, and using logic is not Venus's job. Thinking logically and reaching conclusions is not a task assigned to Venus by God. Therefore, the story says that Lord Vishnu plucked out one of Venus's eyes.

8.4 Love is Blind

Guru Shukracharya, having vision in both eyes, instantly recognizes the hidden intention of the dwarf Brahmin. The presence of both eyes means the ability to understand the difference. Both eyes are symbolic representations of logic, reasoning, and arguments. Such a person concludes only after proper analysis, but having a vision in only one eye means that logic stops, and only feelings remain. That is why it is said that love is blind; it means that love cannot see, it can only be perceived.

Love has only one vision, which means that love can see only one side of any matter and is unable to recognize the hidden aspect. Love cannot understand the hidden intention of the other person because love does not ask for any answer. That is why people get deceived in love because they are unable to differentiate between right and wrong. Therefore, feigning sympathy becomes a weapon to deceive others, and those with a weak mindset often fall victim to it.

8.5 The Meaning of One Eye

Love cannot differentiate, so it cannot understand the difference between the two. The presence of Venus in the horoscope shows that the person cannot differentiate in the matter of that house. In the house where Venus is present, love is present, attraction is present, but there is a lack of ability to differentiate. So, love cannot differentiate between rich and poor; it cannot understand social bondage. Therefore, people refuse to accept logic in love.

Wherever Venus is placed in the horoscope, it is present there with its one eye, which means that the native likes the activities related to that house very much. Wherever the seventh aspect of Venus falls, Venus gives its blind support because one eye of Venus cannot differentiate; love knows no distinction.

The loss of one eye of Venus is a symbolic representation of the fact that Venus has lost its reasoning power and ability to discriminate, and one eye means that only love remains. So, in another sense, when a person shows love towards another person, he closes one of his eyes for a moment, which is commonly called winking.

8.6 Venus is Related to Freshness

Venus is the medium of birth; love gives new birth, where the past is gone forever, and the soul gets a new body. Hence, Venus is related to freshness and novelty. The presence of Venus in a house of the horoscope indicates that the person always likes things related to that house.

Venus is related to freshness, but the life of fresh things is very short. Time throws dust on every fresh thing, and things start to deteriorate. A newborn baby becomes old with time. Because time is destroying things, time is called Kaal in Hindu philosophy. Time makes all fresh things old and removes them; therefore, the presence of Venus in the horoscope demands the utmost attention in that house. Due to a lack of attention, Venus dries up, and the qualities related to that house disappear from the person's life.

8.7 Venus has Sanjeevani Vidya

While time ends life, Venus begins the arrival of a new life. The attraction of Venus is sowing seeds of a new life. Venus is the vehicle on which the soul enters a new womb. Ancient scriptures say that Venus has Sanjeevani Vidya, that is, it puts new life in the dead. A strong Venus indicates that the person puts a new life in deteriorating conditions. Such a person is never disappointed with odd circumstances and always maintains their hope and enthusiasm.

Venus is related to lemon and fresh water. A tired man feels fresh after drinking lemon water; his body becomes alive again. Lemon makes the used and old utensils new again. With the power of the lemon, the utensils start singing again. Similarly, the transit of Venus gives new life to the corresponding house in the horoscope. Therefore, a strong Venus is essential for creation and new birth, because a weak Venus cannot give rise to creativity.

8.8 Venus: No Interest in Conflict and Competition

Venus has no interest in conflict and competition. Love has no interest in conflict and competition because they breed duality. Conflict and competition breed difference, and Venus knows no difference. How can a man compete with the one he loves? Therefore, Venus is interested in giving. Love always gives and never demands, because the one who demands cannot love. We call God the Ocean of Love because He only gives. A mother loves her child and never asks for anything in return. Therefore, parents are considered equal to God for providing life, guidance, and unconditional love.

Where there is demand, there is duality, and where there is duality, there is competition, and where there is competition, there can be no love. Hence, in the presence of Venus, Mars' aggressive energy is suppressed. Therefore, in the presence of a woman, men tend to give up their fighting and behave like gentlemen.

8.9 Relationships and Marriage

Venus is the significator of relationships and marriage. It represents qualities such as cooperation, compromise, and a desire for companionship. Its strength is essential for partnerships, successful and good relationships. An afflicted or weak Venus in the seventh house brings ups and downs in relationships and can sometimes lead to premature separation. It also indicates separation from a relationship after engagement.

8.10 On the Higher Aspect

Love is the feeling of being one in which the feeling of being two disappears. Ancient scriptures say that this world is an extension of God. When the seeker feels one with the whole existence, he drowns in the infinite ocean of Samadhi. Without the help of Venus, no one can enter meditation, so the prevention of semen and the conservation of sexual energy are important. Spirituality is impossible without walking on the path of celibacy.

Venus is the vehicle that helps one reach the destination of Samadhi. Therefore, in astrology, Venus represents the vehicle that helps one reach the destination. Venus means love, which is not limited to the physical body. Love has a broader meaning, the experience of oneness with nature, where all duality ends.

Venus does not want anything in return; the experience of love alone is enough, and that experience cannot be expressed in words. That is why Venus is wordless, and when a person falls in love, he becomes speechless. It becomes difficult to express that experience in words. But that feeling gives birth to music and dance, which is why Venus is associated with music and dance.

The experience of oneness is possible only on the path of love. On this path, all distinctions disappear, and only oneness remains. Attaining the higher aspect of Venus is the ultimate goal. When Venus reaches 27 degrees Pisces in a person's life, every journey ends, and only ecstasy remains.

The feeling of oneness gives birth to the ultimate dance, the feeling of ecstasy gives birth to the ultimate dance, and the entire universe starts dancing. There is no such word to express the feeling of ultimate bliss, but after attaining it, the soul cannot remain silent. This bliss can only be expressed through dance, which is why the Lord is called **Nataraja.**

Chapter 9

Saturn: The Tough Master

9.1 Saturn - The Lord of Justice

Saturn is the lord of justice. As soon as the judge comes to the court, the legal proceedings gain momentum. All the pending cases start getting resolved. Whatever order he gives, everyone has to follow it and there is no way to avoid it. Saturn has a transit period of 30 years and it stays in one sign for 2.5 years. Saturn transit shows that the judge has now entered the court and come to the chair of justice. Therefore, the system gains momentum in the house where Saturn transits. Useless things start getting thrown out and new rules start getting made. The transit of Saturn, whether through a specific house or over a particular planet or upon whichever planet it casts its gaze, it gives birth to a new order, set of rules, or system of management; and whatever has become old and decayed is thrown out forever.

Changes begin to occur in the house and planet on which Saturn's aspect falls. Saturn's transit acts as a catalyst. After getting Saturn's aspect, that planet cannot remain inactive, and new events begin to occur in the person's life. In court, a judge does not cast his gaze on any person without reason, because as soon as the judge's gaze falls on a person, the person becomes disturbed. Therefore, a judge never casts his gaze on a person with whom he has no concern. Similarly, when Saturn's aspect falls on any planet, it cannot remain inactive, and as soon as it becomes active, circumstances in the person's life begin to change.

9.2 Saturn Brings Stability

A common saying about Saturn is that its sight leads a person to downfall, and people become frightened by these words. According to the author, these words should not be taken literally, as they contain a deeper meaning. Saturn is the god of justice and the planet that brings balance and stability. Without stability, there can be no peace, and things cannot last long. If something unstable is being built, it is dangerous for many people. If someone, out of greed, is building something unstable, such as a company or structure, it is dangerous for many people, and Lord Saturn would never allow this to happen.

The god of justice first examines stability and never allows unstable things to stand. Therefore, a popular saying about Saturn is that his glance brings a person down. This means that Saturn's glance never allows anything unstable to stand because it is dangerous. Shani Dev says, first work hard to prepare the foundation and then erect your structure and rise. Saturn brings down all those things that try to rise without building a strong foundation. Saturn's glance examines stability and allows rise only if it passes the test.

According to the author, this is the meaning of "Saturn's aspect brings a person down." Saturn - the planet of balance keeps everything balanced and destroys unstable things without any mercy. Therefore, it is known as a tough master and merciless planet.

It is only through restraint of the mind that determination is born. A fickle and unstable mind lacks determination and stability, and Saturn fosters stability. Therefore, when Saturn decides to undertake a task, it does not rest until it is completed. Stability is born from firm determination. However, its downside is that it breeds stubbornness, and people try to fulfill their desires by controlling others.

9.3 Saturn - The Planet that Changes Fate

Saturn is the controller of fate and shapes destiny through challenges, responsibility, and hard work. Although Saturn is often perceived as a stern master who imposes restrictions and obstacles, its influence ultimately leads to growth and maturity through perseverance and patience. It teaches a person to be determined and move ahead on their path without deviating and to achieve the real goal of life. Saturn always rewards hard work. It ruthlessly removes all those things that have become obsolete and dead.

Saturn's transit brings many transformative events in life and alters a person's destiny. Saturn opens new doors and also closes them. It opens new avenues of fortune and closes many paths forever. Just as a watchman closes a door and then reopens it, Saturn also closes the door and then reopens it. No door can be opened without Shanidev's permission. Saturn locks the door and keeps the key. Therefore, we can say that Saturn is the lock and Saturn is the key.

When the guard locks the door, activity stops, and the next day, people wait for the guard to open the door. When the doors are closed, cleaning cannot be done, and expansion activities cannot take place. Only after the door opens the sun's rays can enter inside, and life can move forward. If Lord Saturn does not allow, the rays of the sun may have to wait at the door for years.

That is why the ancient sutra rightly says – "Sthan Vriddhi Karo Shani" - the presence of Saturn increases the growth of the place. The transit of Saturn plays an important role in life. Saturn removes every adulteration, every falsehood, and every garbage, then only the truth remains. Saturn clears every unnecessary thing in life. That is why it is said that Saturn clears away all the dirt and shows the real truth to the person.

Saturn throws away all the garbage, and if a person is unwilling to let it go, he has to use force. So, Saturn is harsh because it does not allow any kind of garbage to be kept in our lives. When Sade Sati starts, people start getting scared because they are not ready to throw away their garbage, and the conflict starts. They keep collecting it for years and think that there are valuable things in their collection.

But Saturn does not allow us to keep anything that has become waste. So, Saturn removes the ego in Sade Sati because it is completely useless, but people are not ready to throw it away. Then Saturn uses force and removes the cause of ego, so people lose wealth, power, and position in their Sade Sati. The transit of Saturn clears all the garbage, the waste is gone, and now life can move forward.

9.4 Saturn - Gives the Power of Concentration

Strong Saturn gives the power of concentration. Only a determined person can do any concrete work in life. Therefore, a strong Saturn is necessary to do important work in life, because a person with a fickle mind lacks patience, and Saturn provides strong qualities like patience, determination, and concentration. Saturn gives a sense of duty and responsibility. It gives the power of self-control, self-improvement, and hard work. It gives the power to save and accumulate. Therefore, Saturn in the twelfth house limits expenditure, while Jupiter in the twelfth house increases expenditure. When Saturn is placed in an angular or in a trine house, it becomes very strong, but a weak Saturn makes the personality weak.

9.5 The Energy of Saturn Works Gradually and Slowly

Saturn rules our muscles, hair, and nails. It governs our thighs, legs, knees, and colon. Our muscles change, but we don't know when; Our hair and nails grow and we don't know when they grew. This is how the energy of Saturn works - gradually and slowly.

9.6 Saturn - The Planet of Contraction

Saturn is the planet of contraction. It rules solid foundations, immovable properties, and is associated with death. Its energy;

- Tends to pull and freeze.
- Stops movement and makes things solid and stable.
- It gives birth to strong faith, prudence, and loyalty.
- It is related to the past and old age.

Saturn's influence is restrictive, heavy, and long-lasting. It symbolizes discipline, hard work, achievement, and responsibility. It gives rise to challenges, and its slow and steady influence instills patience and endurance, providing the ability to face and overcome major challenges in life. The challenges presented by Saturn refine a person, ultimately leading to profound, lasting results, and through hardships, one learns life's lessons.

The wisdom imparted by Saturn is remembered throughout life.

On the other hand, misdirected Saturn energy creates delays, struggles, worries, and feelings of burden, but if understood and worked with correctly, it creates foundational strength and long-term success.

9.7 The Sign of Saturn

Saturn is the lord of Capricorn and Aquarius, which are the tenth and eleventh signs of the zodiac. The tenth house is related to name, fame, position, occupation, power, and authority, while the eleventh house is related to income, gains, and fulfillment of desires. The presence of Jupiter in the tenth house is an indication that the person will get a job easily, but the presence of Saturn in the tenth house is an indication that the person will have to work hard to achieve success.

If the significators (Karaka) of the tenth house (Mercury, Sun, Saturn, and Jupiter) are in a strong position, they smooth the path of one's career; conversely, if these significators are weak or situated in an inauspicious position, they create obstacles in achieving success. The presence of Sun, Mars, and Mercury helps the person to rise in their career. The conjunction of Saturn and the Moon in the 10th house gives birth to a great mystic.

Saturn's exalted sign is Libra, its debilitated sign is Aries, and its detrimental sign is Cancer. A planet placed in a detrimental sign struggles to express its natural qualities and functions with less vigor. If the cancer sign falls in the 6th, 8th, and 12th houses, then it creates many challenges in life. When Saturn transits in Cancer, many important transformational events take place.

9.8 The Aspects of Saturn

9.8.1 The 3rd Aspect

The third element in the zodiac is a supporting element. The first element is fire, the second is earth, the third is air, and the fourth is water. Fire and air support each other. Therefore, Saturn's third aspect is supportive. Just as air supports fire, Saturn's third aspect is also supportive. However, if there is no fire and no material to fuel the fire, even air cannot be supportive. Saturn's third aspect indicates a smooth flow of energy and activates the things related to that house, but if there is no fire (input), then it cannot support.

The third house is the house of courage. It indicates that with the support of Saturn, a person will display bravery and work to bring balance. Fire expands with the support of air. Similarly, Saturn's third aspect causes things to move. Even if things haven't been moving forward for years, the third aspect of Saturn brings changes. In whatever area or direction, a person has been hesitant to take initiative, and things have remained quiet and subdued for years, Saturn's third aspect gives them the courage to move forward. But Saturn energy is the pull energy. Therefore, one should not take undue advantage of it.

9.8.2 The 7th Aspect

The seventh aspect of any planet indicates support for that house. The support provided by Saturn indicates stability. When any matter related to a house is about to fall, Saturn's seventh aspect protects it. For example, this support can be like a stone protruding from a cliff or a hook tied around the waist that a person can hold on to and prevent a fall. However, too much stability means that things are frozen; therefore, on the negative side, it freezes things. (For details read article 6.14.2)

9.8.3 The 10th Aspect

Saturn's tenth aspect is about control and setting boundaries. The element of the first house is fire, and the element of the tenth house is earth. Fire and earth do not get along; they have a hostile relationship. If we throw mud on fire, it extinguishes the fire. But if we want Earth to support fire, we must control the Earth. When these two elements are under control, they begin to support each other.

For example, clay pots become stronger when baked in the fire. A clay stove helps keep the fire burning. But this is only possible when both elements cooperate with each other. The tenth aspect of Saturn indicates that it can control opposing elements and make them work. Similarly, earth and air do not support each other. But Saturn controls air and makes life easier on Earth.

When the third sign is air, the tenth sign from there is water. When Saturn is in an air sign, its tenth aspect falls on the water sign. Air and water do not cooperate, but Saturn uses air to bring water. Strong winds blow clouds away and bring rain to distant places. Without the help of air, river and ocean water cannot reach far and wide on Earth.

When Saturn is in a water sign, its tenth aspect falls on a fire sign. Fire and water are enemies, but if you want to achieve cooperation, they must be controlled. Controlled fire warms water, and controlled water prevents fire from flaring up.

Under Saturn's control, opposites begin to cooperate and can be used for many purposes. Without control, opposites do not cooperate, and the animosity between them causes things to spiral out of control. The goal of Saturn's tenth aspect is to fully control two opposing elements and harness them to achieve a goal.

Saturn's tenth aspect represents the control through which even impossible tasks can be made possible. Therefore, the tenth house is the house of action, where a person makes the impossible possible through their hard work. The tenth aspect forces even the opposing forces to cooperate. Saturn represents bondage, whose gaze binds a person. Therefore, Saturn is considered the most important planet in astrology, from whose grip no one can escape.

When Saturn is exalted in Libra, its tenth aspect falls on Cancer, making even impossible tasks possible. Where Saturn's tenth aspect falls, unexpected events occur in life. In the house where transiting Saturn's tenth aspect falls, a long-closed door opens, like a hammer breaking an old lock. Therefore, the tenth aspect of Saturn brings significant changes in life.

The Aspect of Saturn

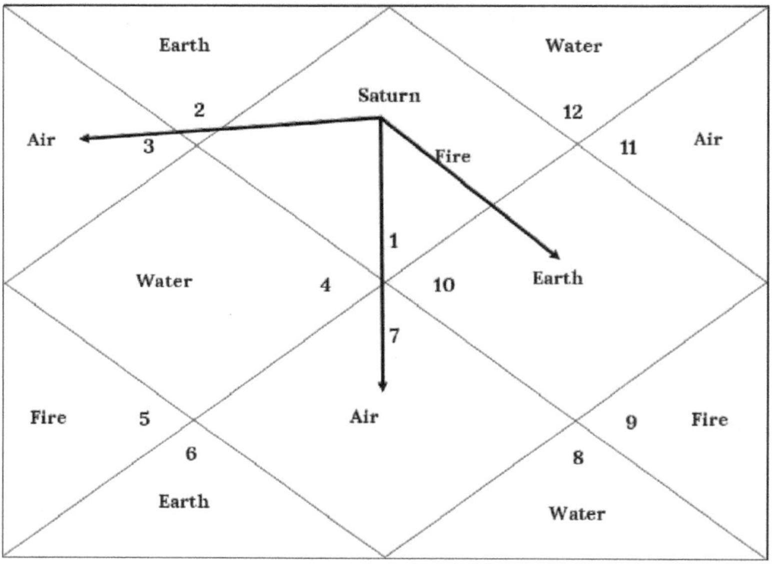

9.9 Saturn, Struggle and Growth

Saturn is a tough master who doesn't give anything easily because he knows that people don't appreciate what comes without hard work. Saturn demands discipline, responsibility, and dedication for success. Growth is impossible without facing the struggles generated by Saturn. Therefore, the ancient scriptures say, "Sthaan Vriddhi Karo Shani" i.e. "Saturn causes growth in the place it occupies".

But Saturn's influence isn't about ease; it's about pressure that builds strength. Therefore, it's not just about enduring pain and struggle; it's about transformation through challenge. Just as practice hones skills, difficulties foster maturity. When a person overcomes difficulties and moves forward, a brilliant talent is born and new avenues of growth open up. Therefore, Saturn represents perseverance, and when used correctly, such a person is not daunted by difficulties. Even if they fall many times, they get back up again.

Those who seek quick advancement often abandon struggle and become interested in shortcuts (Rahu), seeking results without hard work. However, such success is unsustainable and quickly brings one down. Saturn fosters maturity through challenges, delays, and limitations, clearing the path to long-term success. Saturn's struggles strengthen a person, enhancing their spirit and enabling them to achieve long-lasting success.

Therefore, Saturn's aspect creates fear in people and is considered a difficult aspect because Saturn tests patience and stability. If a person is building a weak structure or trying to take undue advantage of it, Saturn's aspect brings down such a structure. Saturn never allows a weak pillar to stand. Therefore, when Saturn's aspect begins, many things in a person's life begin to change. Saturn brings struggle, and this is necessary for development and growth.

Growth under Saturn is slow and deliberate, leading to solid and lasting success. By facing difficulties, one learns patience and the ability to handle difficult situations, which are essential for long-term wisdom. Saturn's energy rewards perseverance rather than shortcuts, and one is forced to confront the truth. Therefore, Saturn's struggle paves the way for long-lasting progress.

Chapter 10

Rahu & Ketu

Rahu and Ketu are both known as invisible and mysterious planets in astrology. According to mythology, Lord Vishnu beheaded a demon named Swarnabhanu while he was sitting by the side of the gods at the time of distributing amrita (nectar). At that time, Swarnabhanu knew that the gods were not going to fulfill their promise of equitable distribution of nectar. He changed his entire outfit, began to look like a deity, and sat on the side where the deity was sitting to drink the nectar. But the Sun and the Moon recognized that he is not a deity, he is a demon, and they informed Lord Vishnu.

Immediately, Lord Vishnu beheaded him, but before that, he had drunk a few drops of nectar, which is why he became immortal. His head is called Rahu, and his headless body becomes Ketu.

Sun, Earth, and Moon play an important role in giving birth to these two planets, which are known as shadow the results associated with them cannot be predicted accurately.

10.1 Rahu

Rahu - the north node of the Moon is a shadowy planet. The direction of Rahu is South-West and stays 18 months in a sign. The caste of Rahu is Mleccha (outcaste), and it represents all foreign elements like a foreign land, foreign caste, foreign people, etc. Rahu represents those reptiles having poison in their mouths, like snakes, while Ketu represents those insects and creatures having poison in their tails, like scorpions.

The mythology is very important to understand the characteristics of Rahu. Just like Swarnabhanu had an intense desire to drink the nectar at any cost, Rahu signifies passion, obsession, and madness. To achieve this burning desire, he changed his face, changed his clothes, left the side of demons, joined the side of devatas, and took big risks with only one goal, or better, we can say with only one obsession – "I want this nectar at any cost," and he achieved it. But after achieving this, he lost his body shape.

The behavior of the person having a strong influence on Rahu is also the same. They are extremely obsessed with achieving their desire. For that purpose, they can cross any limit and don't care about the outcome or suffering. Just as Swarnabhanu lost the shape of his body in the end, similarly, a person following the path of his obsession has to lose a lot from his life. One day, he will get what he wants, but for this, he will have to pay a huge price, just like Swarnabhanu paid by getting his head chopped off.

Mythology says that the Sun and the Moon recognized the demon sitting by the side of the gods and informed Lord Vishnu. After that, Sun and Moon became strong enemies of Rahu and Ketu. Eclipse is caused due to the transit of Rahu & Ketu, and they have complete power to engulf the Sun and Moon.

Sun and Moon represent our soul and mind. It means that if you run after your desire, your soul and mind will become weak, your vision will become blurred, and you will not be able to identify the truth. The smoke of desires will gradually surround you, and it will take over your soul and mind. But if your soul and mind are strong, then you can recognize the illusion created by Rahu.

The person who has a strong Sun and Moon can easily catch the hidden motive of the mischievous persons and keep himself away from all these. This is one of the many reasons we worship the Sun and the Moon in Hindu culture, so that our spirit and mind are strong and not eclipsed by material desire in the mundane world.

Rahu has only a mouth but no body. It indicates that a person with a strong influence of Rahu has a great desire but does not have the ability to digest it. Rahu always thinks about the future, and its position in the horoscope indicates that the person wants to experience things that he has not had till now. Rahu means imbalance, mistakes, where a person learns from their experience. Rahu is such a power that does not listen to anyone's advice and is ready to cross any limit to fulfill his intense desire. Such natives do not care about the result, even if their head is cut off like Swarnabhanu.

Rahu is an airy and lawless planet. Rahu does not like any boundaries. A person having a strong influence of Rahu behaves the same. They don't want any control over themselves, they are ready to break any rule, and sometimes their behavior is over expansive. They don't like any questions, and they don't want to give any explanations. They wander here and there like air and waste their time and energy.

10.2 Ketu

Ketu - the south node, is the shadow planet of sudden and unexpected things. It represents the experiences of our past lives, which we learned at a very high level and with mastery. It also represents a rigid and critical mindset where perfection is the highest goal at any cost.

The symbol of Ketu is a flag that always stands vertically, indicating the direction of the planet. A flag represents victory, but victory is not easy; victory on the battlefield is after much bloodshed and great sacrifices. The position of Ketu indicates that the native will get a victory after a lot of hard work and great sacrifice. Ketu provides clairvoyance and wisdom, but after wanderings and sufferings.

A strong Ketu blessed the native with powerful insights. It gives a power of intense concentration and deep penetration. This also represents vaccination, where medicine is injected into the body. Ketu represents intuition, isolation, mediation, deep research, scientific jobs, drilling activities, etc. It belongs to those jobs where a person works with full concentration to achieve their goal; the person leaves the rest of the world and forgets everything. A strong Ketu is necessary to sit in meditation for long hours. Ketu is a planet of seclusion and has no interest in the material world; the higher aspect of Ketu is salvation (Moksha).

<u>Sun and Moon's Path Intersection</u>

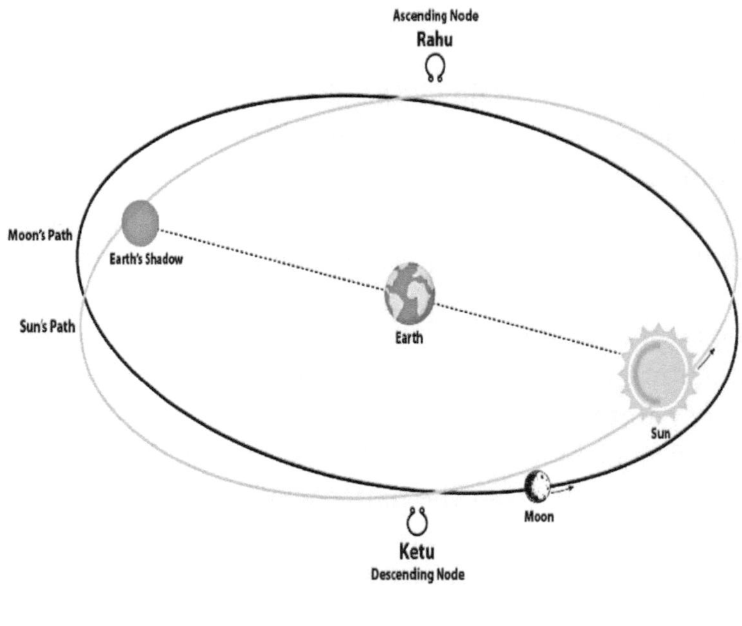

Chapter 11

Transit of Saturn Over Natal Rahu and Ketu

11.1 Transit of Saturn Over Natal Rahu

Rahu forces the person to run in the material world to fulfill desire. The placement of Rahu in a horoscope indicates that the person has to achieve those things in life that he has not yet achieved. Therefore, Rahu represents the race to achieve unfulfilled desires. Rahu is ambitious, and the transit or aspect of Saturn on natal Rahu forces the person to fulfill the unfulfilled desires. Rahu is bold and can break any rules or boundaries and cross the limit to fulfill his desire.

At the time when Saturn transits or aspects over natal Rahu, the person is ready to face challenges and take bold steps in life. But it also gives rise to unexpected events, and the person's life changes completely. The aspect of the transiting Saturn on the natal Rahu forces the person to run around.

Saturn brings limitations, hates haste, and does work only after careful consideration. Rahu is hasty and does not like to wait. Rahu wants quick success, and when Saturn delays the work, the person starts getting frustrated and starts looking for other, easier ways to fulfill his desire. Saturn rewards consistent effort, honesty, and dedication, and these words do not matter to Rahu. Hence, during this time, the person becomes selfish and uses unfair means to achieve what he wants.

Saturn symbolizes discipline, and Rahu represents out-of-the-box thinking. Hence, people do not like to follow rules to get what they want. They are interested in taking shortcuts to achieve their goals. It also indicates involvement in wrongdoings where the native may get involved in secretive and unlawful activities. Saturn represents secrecy, and Rahu enhances it; hence, the native wants to fulfill his desires quickly by engaging in conspiracies, smuggling, and illegal activities.

Saturn teaches patience, and Rahu is impatient. Rahu's restless nature makes a person rush to do everything as quickly as possible. They are in a hurry to fulfill their material desires, so they are not concerned about the ways and means to achieve them. Saturn is slow, and Rahu wants success at any cost and is ready to do anything to get what he wants.

Rahu is an expert in painting rosy pictures, which are nothing but an illusion. Saturn clears every dirt and shows the true picture of life. It indicates that the person has to learn hard lessons in life, and Saturn brings the person down to earth. This transit creates restlessness, stress, and anxiety in life.

11.2 Transit of Saturn Over Natal Ketu

Ketu is a planet of separation and sudden events. A person has to face sudden changes in their life related to the matter of the concerned house. Ketu indicates new beginnings. When Saturn transits over Ketu, one chapter in life is closed forever, and life changes to a new phase. After the completion of Saturn transit, i.e., after 2.5 years, a person's life is completely changed from their previous life.

Saturn represents dry wood, and Ketu represents fire. When dry wood comes in contact with fire, it immediately burns. When Saturn in transit crosses over natal Ketu, fire burns in the respective house. During this time, the person has to face many challenges in life, and the situation demands hard work for success.

During this time, something is separating from life, and something new is coming. During this time, there is a period of transition when the past has to go but is not yet gone, and the future is coming but has not yet come. Therefore, challenges are high during this period, and the individual experiences a great deal of restlessness.

Ketu is the planet of separation. When Saturn aspects Ketu in transit, then the separating energy of Ketu gets activated, and something gets separated from the native's life forever.

For example, if Ketu is placed in the 10th house and Saturn in transit indicates that the job or work profile or workplace is going to change during this transit. If Ketu is placed in the 11th house when Saturn transits over Ketu, it is possible that the person's relationship with his old friend will be closed forever, or his source of income will change. When Ketu is placed in the fourth house, the person may change their home.

On the higher aspect, Saturn's association with Ketu represents the burning of dry wood, and this fire can take the person to the heights of spirituality.

Chapter 12

Planetary Lordship of Nakshatras

12.1 Nakshatra of Ketu

Ketu is the lord of three Nakshatras: 1) Ashwini, 2) Magha, 3) Mula.

1) Ashwini: This is the first nakshatra that indicates initiation and beginning. Ketu is a headless and shadow planet. The head represents ego, and the headless ruler indicates modesty and humbleness of the person. Ashwini is the first nakshatra and signifies the beginning of a new cycle. Hence, the rulership of this nakshatra is given to Ketu, which signifies separation from the past as the new can begin only after the old ends. The number of Ketu is seven, and in Hindu mythology, the Sun God travels on a chariot drawn by seven horses. Sun means a new beginning; hence, the Sun becomes exalted in this nakshatra.

2) Magha: This nakshatra is related to the seeds received from the ancestors. It has a deep connection with creation, and these people can start something new in life with the help of old seeds. Where the previous nakshatra Ashlesha ends, Gandanta exists, and after that Magha begins. After every Gandanta, Ketu nakshatra begins, which indicates the beginning of a new cycle. Magha is related to the past, where everything has gone, but the seeds are saved for the future. Therefore, these people can quickly understand things related to the past and use them for the future. Since every seed needs extreme care and not even a single seed can be allowed to go to waste, extreme care is required to start a new cycle with a deep understanding of the past.

3) Mula: It is related to the roots or foundation, and the root is the first essential thing that creates a base for a large tree. Any new beginning requires a strong foundation, and from where the Mula starts, the watery sign ends, and fiery signs begin, and there is no relation between water and fire. Hence, Ketu, the planet of separation or new beginning, is the lord of this Nakshatra. Roots indicate a beginning; therefore, Mula natives do not hesitate to destroy old beliefs and thoughts. They immediately cut those things that have become irrelevant, but others are carrying them in the name of tradition.

The following are the differences between the nakshatras of Ketu;

- **Ashwini** – A new beginning with courage

- **Magha** – A new beginning from seeds collected in the past
- **Mula** - A new beginning by strengthening the roots

12.2 Nakshatra of Venus

Venus is the lord of three Nakshatras: 1) Bharani, 2) Purva Phalguni, 3) Purva Ashadha.

1) Bharani: The symbol of this nakshatra is Yoni (Vagina). It is a female sexual organ, and it is the source of existence. It is a way of birth where a sperm enters and takes the shape of a baby. Venus, the planetary lord of this Nakshatra, is related to the reproductive part of the body. Venus is the lord of sexual energy, which has the power to transform and give new birth.

2) Purva Phalguni: Venus is the lord of this Nakshatra, who is the lord of the reproductive organs in the body. It is the sexual energy that compels a person to have children. Children are our creation, and without sexual energy, it is not possible. The lordship of Venus indicates that Purva Phalguni person has the best quality to create something new. A beautiful creation is possible only when the mind is completely relaxed, and the body follows the direction given by the mind.

A weak mind and a tired body cannot create anything. Hence, the energy of the Nakshatra compels the person to rejuvenate, and the best creation in the world is seen when the person is completely relaxed and calm. Every moment, the entire existence is giving birth anew, and reproduction is ongoing incessantly. Therefore, this energy has strong potential to give birth to new and innovative things in life.

3) Purva Ashadha: This nakshatra has a profound connection with water. Water has strong healing properties, and when it starts raining, optimism for life starts among the people. The lordship of the nakshatra is given to 'Venus', which represents fresh drinking water that energizes us and boosts our body functions.

The water of Purva Ashadha is not like the Ardra water, which wreaks havoc; it is the sweet water of the rain that people enjoy. This water gets stored in various reservoirs, which are used by the people throughout the year. This water gives us life, this water gives freshness to our face, and is used to wash away dirt and clean everything. Venus is an attractive planet. When the dirt is removed, things become clean and attractive.

Venus is a gentle and non-aggressive feminine energy. There are differences in all three Venusian energies.

- **Bharani** - This energy is to nourish and protect
- **Purva Phalguni** – This energy is for creation with joy
- **Purva Ashadha** - This is the energy for rejuvenation

12.3 Nakshatra of Sun

Sun is the lord of three Nakshatras: 1) Krittika, 2) Uttara Phalguni, 3) Uttara Ashadha.

1) Krittika: This energy is a very high, fiery energy. It is very sharp and has a strong ability to penetrate deeply. The nature of this energy is "Sharp and Soft," and the nature of the Sun is sharp and soft, and both are necessary to maintain the environment on Earth. The Sun in the summer season is sharp, but the same Sun during the winter season is soft.

A king cannot remain heated all the time; for a declaration of war, heat is necessary, but for signing a peaceful agreement, a soft nature is required. The energy of the nakshatra favors cutting and burning for creation. It is a protective energy, and when it comes to protection, this energy never hesitates to cut something.

2) Uttara Phalguni: This energy provides the ability to choose the best, which is helpful in development and growth. This energy keeps a proper balance in each and every activity of life. These individuals are very courageous and have leadership qualities. Lord Sun bestows the native with courage and the quality of showing light to others.

3) Uttara Ashadha: The focus of this nakshatra is always on victory, and only an enlightened person can be victorious forever. Worshipping the Sun dispels all the darkness of a person, and only light remains. The Sun indicates an adventurous person who is never afraid to go it alone. It also indicates a committed and conscientious person. Uttara Ashadha indicates a charismatic personality; once they accept a task, they never leave it before its completion.

The following are the differences between the nakshatras of the Sun;

• **Krittika** - Both sharp and soft qualities are present here, but only one comes to the surface at a time.

• **Uttara Phalguni** - This energy works for development and growth through hard work. This nakshatra represents the quality of action.

• **Uttara Ashadha** - This energy works to become victorious at any cost.

12.4 Nakshatra of Moon

Moon is the lord of three Nakshatras: 1) Rohini, 2) Hasta, 3) Shravana.

1) Rohini: Rohini is a very soft energy and cannot become harsh at any point in time. When the moon rises above the horizon, all soft activities begin to take shape, and people take an interest in pleasurable activities. Dancing, music, and singing begin, and aggression disappears. The energy of love starts spreading all around, and creativity starts happening, and the great creativity of the world continues with the energy of the Sun and Moon. So, Rohini comes after Kritika, and the energy of the Moon comes after the Sun.

Every great creation begins in deep silence, and the Moon represents our mind. When a person's mind is completely calm, they are capable of doing creative work. Only a calm person can do creation because a restless mind cannot catch subtle nuances, and when the mind is unable to catch the finer details, it is unable to understand the art. When the light of the moon is high, the power of creation is high, so great things are done on the full moon day. Lord Buddha attained enlightenment on the full moon day.

2) Hasta: The Sanskrit word Hasta means hand, so this nakshatra has a strong relation with the hands. The proper functioning of a hand requires all five fingers with a palm; it indicates a perfect grip that means full control. All fingers work simultaneously to achieve one objective, which indicates unity, strength, and cooperation. An open hand indicates receptivity and acceptance. With an open hand, a person welcomes another person and shows cordial behaviour. The rulership of the Moon indicates an extremely soft and polite nature of the person, who never wants to indulge in any type of quarrel.

3) Shravana: The word Shravana comes from the Sanskrit word 'Shrava', which means hearing. Therefore, Shravana means the act of hearing or that which is heard. When one thing collides with another, sound is produced; that is, two are needed to produce sound, and this world is the sound of two. The energy of this Nakshatra pulls all the sound towards itself. If any sound is produced by a collision, then Shravana hears it immediately. The lordship of the Moon indicates a non-aggressive person.

The differences among all three Moon nakshatras are;

- **Rohini** – Creation through love
- **Hasta** - Creation by intellect

- **Shravana** - Creation through receptivity

12.5 Nakshatra of Mars

Mars is the lord of three Nakshatras: 1) Mrigashira, 2) Chitra, 3) Dhanishta.

1) Mrigashira: It is the seeking energy, and such a person seeks every hidden thing, and the most hidden one is the Supreme Soul. The soul searches for it everywhere and does not find it, yet this Nakshatra keeps on giving energy and does not sit idle. Because such a discovery requires incessant energy, Mars is the lord of this Nakshatra.

2) Chitra: The lordship of Mars indicates that this energy works for protection and keeps away every evil thing. Whosoever is looking for protection, Chitra is always ready to help. Mars means tamas and desire. It doesn't have only one meaning; that desire for material pleasure, tamas, also means darkness and seclusion.

The desire to accomplish goals and excel requires constant energy; such a person is not easily discouraged and never sits idly by. They are not satisfied with simple things and are not ready to give up their will; they believe in hard work and have the ability to do more than others. Mars does not indicate a quarrelsome person, but it shows the fighting spirit against all odds to achieve the goal.

3) Dhanishta: In a work where many forces are affecting the outcome, it is very difficult to coordinate, because the difference of even a microsecond makes a difference.

It requires a deep understanding of every procedure and flow of every action. Such efficiency is possible when a person fully understands the pattern of timing, repetition, and required spacing of each element. When to create harmony in the mundane world is difficult, so what about the creation of harmony in the inner world where multiple desires simultaneously force, it requires a lot of energy. Therefore, Mars is assigned as the lord of this nakshatra.

The differences among all three Mars nakshatras are as follows;

- **Mrigashira** - A relentless seeking energy
- **Chitra** - Excellence and radiance
- **Dhanishtha** - Establishing harmony through the use of pressure and force

12.6 Nakshatra of Rahu

Rahu is the lord of three Nakshatras: 1) Ardra, 2) Swati, 3) Shatabhisha.

1) Ardra: Rahu doesn't like to follow the rules, having the ability to break any barrier, the lordship of this nakshatra is provided to Rahu. The presence of Rahu indicates inconsistency, i.e., the functioning of this energy is not smooth. The water related to this Nakshatra is not ordinary, silent water; it is extremely powerful, like the flood that does not follow any rules and breaks all barriers. Water has the quality of purification, and it takes away all the dirt. It is a very powerful transformational energy that brings significant changes in the life of the person.

2) Swati: Swati symbolizes the ultimate level of purity. Hence, the energy of this Nakshatra churns and works to achieve the supreme. It is said that a special bird named Chatak (Jacobin Cuckoo) drinks only the rainwater that falls in the Swati Nakshatra. Even if the bird is thirsty, it does not open its beak to any other water; it never drinks water from lakes, ponds, or rivers, and quenches its thirst only when it rains. In the same way, people of this nakshatra believe in purity at any cost, and they keep patience for the outcome.

This energy works to get the purest things, but it is not easy. To become a master or a perfectionist, one has to learn many things and correct mistakes. It is very difficult to recognize the impurities of our mind, then work hard to remove it, for this strong willpower is required. When a person is in the process of getting rid of all the impurities that are causing obstruction, no order is needed to remove them. Hence, Rahu, the planet of disorder, compels such a person to seek perfection, and he uses all means to achieve his objective. The planets in the Swati Nakshatra indicate that the life of such a person is not normal. They have to go through many disturbances till they become perfectionists.

3) Shatabhisha: Rahu is a turbulent planet, creating disorder and chaos to achieve its objective. This indicates that this energy does not rest until they solve the problem or achieve their objective. The mythological story states that Rahu did everything to get the nectar;

similarly, such a person does everything to achieve his objective and never remains silent. The question always revolves around in his mind, and he is busy finding the solution.

The differences among all three Rahu nakshatras are;

- **Ardra** - Cleansing and transformation through beating by soaking in water
- **Swati** - Purification through churning
- **Shatabhisha** - Achieving the objective at any cost

12.7 Nakshatra of Jupiter

Jupiter is the lord of three Nakshatras: 1) Punarvasu, 2) Vishakha, 3) Purva Bhadrapada.

1) Punarvasu: The word Punarvasu means 'Bright again', 'Afresh again', or 'Excellent again'. The energy of this nakshatra works for the power to regain wealth and objectives. The symbol of Punarvasu is "Quiver of arrows," which indicates that if one arrow misses the target, then another will hit, and the process will go on until the target has been achieved. Only the planet that provides endless hope can become the lord of this nakshatra. Hence, Jupiter is the lord of this nakshatra.

2) Vishakha: The word Vishakha means a branch that is forked or divided into two parts. It also means a two-way path is merged into a single path and indicates one point or one direction. This is the place where the energy level is very high, and such energy should always be in the right hands. Dealing with such energy requires both wisdom and benevolence. Even poison becomes medicine in the hands of a worthy person. High energy and great knowledge can harm the hands of the wrong person. Therefore, Jupiter is the ruler of this Nakshatra.

3) Purva Bhadrapada: The energy of this nakshatra is like a hurricane, and the vortex forms the shape of "One Footed God", ready to destroy everything that comes in his way. It is extreme and destructive energy. Therefore, the purpose of such destruction must be noble. Hence, the energy works for constructive destruction. Such a fierce and destructive energy can be controlled only by the planet of benevolence. Therefore, Jupiter is the ruler of this nakshatra.

The energy for all three Jupiter nakshatra works for creation. The following is the difference between these energies:

- **Punarvasu -** Creation through repetition
- **Vishakha -** Creation through transformation
- **Purva Bhadrapada -** Creation after destruction

12.8 Nakshatra of Saturn

Saturn is the lord of three Nakshatras: 1) Pushya, 2) Anuradha, 3) Uttara Bhadrapada.

1) Pushya: Pushya means the one who nourishes, the one who gives energy and strength. This nakshatra is related to caring, nurturing, and teaching. As a cow gives us milk from its teat, they always take interest in nurturing the mental, emotional, physical, and spiritual aspects of life. Such persons always do everything for the betterment of others, and they gain fame and popularity by their gentle behavior and knowledge. These activities require enough maturity. Therefore, the lordship of this nakshatra is given to Saturn.

2) Anuradha: The energy of this nakshatra gives the power to fight adverse circumstances with fewer resources. They always keep smiling, speak in a sweet voice, and do not panic in any situation in life. Their mind is always ready to find a way out of the problem. When someone does not believe in their victory, doubts their ability, and leaves them, then the person fights alone and emerges victorious. Therefore, Saturn, the Lord of patience, is the lord of this nakshatra.

3) Uttara Bhadrapada: Uttara means latter, left, or where everything has an answer. Bhadra means auspicious, and Pada means feet, which represent stability and strength. When the answer is found, all questions cease to exist. The energy of this constellation works to find solutions, and the search continues till the answer is found. Legs represent stability, and stability requires balance. Hence, the lord of balance, 'Saturn', is the ruler of this nakshatra.

The energies of the three Saturn nakshatras prove the adage "slow and steady wins the race." The differences between them are as follows:

• **Pushya –** A very hard-working and diligent person who has to do everything to win in the odd circumstances.

• **Anuradha** - Fighting all difficulties and overcoming every obstacle in life, and still maintaining a smile on the face with a sweet voice.

• **Uttara Bhadrapada -** This compassionate, deep, and productive energy can bring about change from the roots.

12.9 Nakshatra of Mercury

Mercury is the lord of three Nakshatras: 1) Ashlesha, 2) Jyeshtha, 3) Revati.

1) Ashlesha - The word Ashlesha means to embrace, entwine, adhere, and have a close connection. Ashlesha is associated with poison, and poison produces heat. This star falls in the water sign Cancer, and the water calms the heat. Water represents a state of calm mind, so the mind of an Ashlesha person is usually calm unless it is provoked; the heat is buried in the water, due to which their anger is hidden and can come out at any time. Ashlesha has the quality of bending, and bending signifies diplomacy.

2) Jyeshtha - The Sanskrit word Jyeshtha means the eldest. Jyeshtha signifies progress and rise, which is possible only through intelligence. These people first secure their position before acting on the next step. They protect their family, friends, and subordinates.

3) Revati - The word Revati comes from the Sanskrit word Revat, which means wealthy and prosperous. Mercury, being the lord, indicates that naive state of mind where the person has seen through the fallacies of all tricks and is no longer interested in any tricks. He has again attained the innocence of children and become lord of the supreme wisdom. These people are very social and always behave politely. They have a refined nature and show proper etiquette and manners. They look for joy, prefer light jokes in their discussion, and remain optimistic in difficult situations in life. It is always their instinct to nurture others, so they are always ready to provide necessary help to others.

The energy of all three Mercury nakshatras is related to intelligence.

- **Ashlesha** - Signifies diplomacy
- **Jyeshtha** - Signifies preparation, planning, and progress.
- **Revati** - Signifies childlike dynamism and flexibility.

Bibliography

Brihat Parashara Hora Sastra by Maharshi Parasara

Brihat Jatak, Translation by Prof. P.S. Sastri, Rajan Publications, New Delhi

Jatak Parijat, Translation by V. Subramanya Sastri, Rajan Publications, New Delhi

Phaladeepika, Translation by V. Subrahmanya Sastri, Aruna Press, Bangalore

Bhavartha Ratnakar, Translation by B.V. Raman, UBS Publishers, New Delhi,

ABC of Indian Astrology, Prof. (Dr.) Nimai Banerjee, Published by Mrs. Kanti Banerjee, Cuttak

Fundamental Principals of Astrology, by Prof. K.S. Krishnamurti

Scientific Hindu Astrology Vol 1 &2 by P.S. Sastri

Hora Sara, by Prithuyasas (Translation by R. Santhanam)

Rationale of Astrology – Sri Dandapani Panda – Bhubaneswar, Orissa

Saravali Vol 1 &2 (Translation by R. Santhanam)

Secrets of Predicting Dasha Results by Dr. Nimai Banerjee, Bhagyalipi Publications, Cuttack

Techniques of Predicting Future by Dr. Nimai Banerjee, Bhagyalipi Publications, Cuttack

Planetary Behavior & Human Life, Bhagyalipi Publications, Cuttack

Commentary on Sapta Rishi Nadi by J.N. Bhasin

https://www.wisdomlib.org/hinduism/book/mundaka-upanishad-shankara-bhashya/d/doc145081.html > Accessed on July25, 2025

https://www.holy-bhagavad-gita.org/chapter/10/verse/8/ > Accessed on July27, 2025

https://auromere.wordpress.com/2010/03/18/sri-aurobindo-and-the-mother-on-astrology/ > Accessed on July28, 2025

https://sri-aurobindo.co.in/workings/sa/17/0072_e.htm> Accessed on July28, 2025

About The Author

Ajay Srivastava is the founder of lotuswisdom.in and holds 'Bachelor of Science' from Deen Dayal Upadhyay Gorakhpur University, Gorakhpur (UP) and 'Masters Programme in International Business' from PSG Institute of Management, Coimbatore (Tamil Nadu).

He has extensive experience in the capital market as a Lead Analyst, Investment Banker, Consultant, and Advisor in identifying investment opportunities and formulating strategies. In his career, he has written various research notes and has done in-depth research from a commercial and financing point of view in multiple deals. With diverse industry experience and wide understanding, he started imparting his knowledge in the industry since 2013.

He has deep knowledge of graphology and since childhood he is very much interested in analyzing a person by handwriting and has analyzed the handwriting of hundreds of persons in his life.

He is very much passionate to learn about astrology and palmistry in deep and has completed 'JyotirVid' and 'JyotirVisharad' in Astrology from Bharatiya Vidya Bhavan, Mumbai. His various research articles have been published in the renowned magazine "The Astrological eMagazine" and "Planets & Forecast".

Email ID: ajay.vastav@gmail.com

Web Site: http://www.lotuswisdom.in/

Books Written by the Author

1. Psychology and Investment

2. Vedic Astrology: The Light of Wisdom

3. Midlife Crisis: An Astrological Appraoch

4. Jupiter: The Planet of Fortune

5. The Joy of Creation and Success

6. The Light of Nakshatras

7. Sun: The Supreme Creator

8. Astrology & Predictions

9. Animal Symbols of Nakshatras

10. Astrology & Profession

11. Rahu & Ketu: The Invisible & Mysterious Planets

12. Planets & Human Life

Astrology Courses

1. Vedic Astrology for Beginners {Level – 1 (Basics)}

Module – 1: Basics of Astrology

Introduction; The Zodiac; Elements

Module – 2: Signs

Meaning of the Signs, Elements of the Signs, Qualities of the Signs, Odd and Even Signs, Sheershodaya & Prishtodaya Signs, Direction, Colors, Caste, Fruitful and Barren Signs, Masculine & Feminine Signs, Places, Other Major Qualities

Module – 3: Houses

Meaning of the 12 Houses, Types and Classifications of Houses

Module – 4: Planets

Planets and their Characteristics, Planetary Relationship, Exaltation, Debilitation & Mooltrikona, Natural Karakas, Karakas in Jaimini Astrology

Module – 5: Planets in Groups

Natural Benefic and Malefic Planets, Gender; Color; Caste; Guna and Places; Planet and Tastes; Nature of Planet; Elements; Metals; Age; Cloth and Height; Vegetable and Fruits; Physical Constituents and Tendency; Maturity Age of Planets; Planetary Aspects; Seasons

Module – 6: Planetary Strengths and Weaknesses

Strength of Planets based on its degrees, Direction; Direction Strength; Maran Karaka Sthana; Yog Karaka; Vargottam Planet; Shadabala

Module – 7: Retrograde and Combust Planet, Gandanta

2. <u>Vedic Astrology for Beginners {Level – 2 (Advanced)}</u>

Module 1: Vimshottari Dasha System

Nakshatra and Planetary Lordship, Change of Dasa and Results

Module 2: Basics of Nakshatra

Deity, Animal Symbol, Caste, Activity, Gana, Guna, Gender

Module 3: Important Yogas

Know the 30 most important astrological combinations

Module 4: Ashtakvarga

Interpretation of Ashtakvarga Table

Module 5: Transit of Planets and their impact

Understand the effect of transit of Jupiter, Saturn, Rahu-Ketu

Module 6: Planets and Profession

Identify the influence of the planet and the direction of profession

Module 7: Weak Planets and Remedies

Identify the signal of weak planets and useful remedies

Module 8: Key Steps to Chart Interpretation

Course Offerings:

- 30 hours of live sessions (Level 1 & Level 2)
- Learn various astrological concepts with practical examples
- Mode - Online Classes
- Recordings available

3. Nakshatra Course

Knowledge of Nakshatra is very important in astrology, without it one cannot understand how energy works and what will be the result of the transit of planets. Do not limit yourself to the movement of planets, explore the world of Nakshatra and understand the hidden secrets.

What You'll Learn

- How the knowledge of Nakshatra helps to understand the characteristics and negative traits of the person
- Effect of transit of planets and time of activation
- Meaning of each symbol and its influence
- Influence of the associated animal on the personality of the person
- When to start a new venture and when not to go ahead
- Related Profession
- Understand each concept with logic

Course Offerings:

- 60 hours of live sessions
- Learn various astrological concepts with practical examples
- Mode - Online Classes, Recordings available
- Medium - English

Contact Us:

Mobile No.: +91 9867581379

Email ID: ajay.vastav@gmail.com

Blog: https://lotuswisdomonline.blogspot.com/

4. A Course on Animal Symbols of Nakshatras

In the ancient scriptures, a total of 14 animals are related to the 27 nakshatras, and the behavior of every person is limited to these 14 animals. To understand the various merits and demerits of a person, it is necessary to understand the different characteristics of these animals.

How to Utilize Such Knowledge

• You will be surprised to know that these animals decide whom we form a relationship in our life.

• These animals determine our relationships with our friends, our spouse, our partners, our juniors and superiors.

• This knowledge helps to channelize your energy in pursuit of higher goals in life.

• The human mind is a very complex creation and it is difficult to say why a person behaves in a certain way and why his behavior changes. Knowledge of animal traits can provide proper guidance in this regard.

Course Offerings:

- 30 hours of live sessions
- Learn various astrological concepts with practical examples
- Mode - Online Classes
- Recordings available

Images of English Books

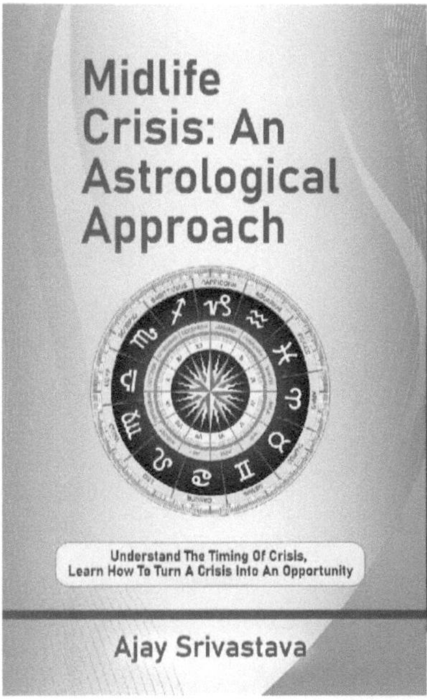
Midlife Crisis: An Astrological Approach
Understand The Timing Of Crisis, Learn How To Turn A Crisis Into An Opportunity
Ajay Srivastava

PSYCHOLOGY AND INVESTMENT
The Art of Investing in Stocks with an Explanation of Human Psychology
AJAY SRIVASTAVA

The Joy of Creation and Success
Ajay Srivastava

Astrology & Predictions
Ajay Srivastava

Animal Symbols
of
Nakshatras
Ajay Srivastava

Astrology
&
Profession
Astrological Principles Behind Career
Selection, Downfall and Resurrection
Ajay Srivastava

Rahu & Ketu
The Invisible and Mysterious Planets
An Extensive Research Work to Demystify
the Mystery of Lunar Nodes
Ajay Srivastava

Planets
&
Human Life
A Research Work on The Impact of
The Nine Planets on Human Life
Ajay Srivastava

Notes

Notes

www.ingramcontent.com/pod-product-compliance
Ingram Content Group UK Ltd.
Pitfield, Milton Keynes, MK11 3LW, UK
UKHW041313190726
13845UKWH00025B/247

9 789357 595070